FEEDING *a* FAMILY

Sarah Waldman
photographs by Elizabeth Cecil

FEEDING *a* FAMILY

Simple and Healthy
Weeknight Meals the Whole
Family Will Love

ROOST BOOKS
BOULDER
2018

Roost Books
An imprint of Shambhala Publications, Inc.
4720 Walnut Street
Boulder, Colorado 80301
roostbooks.com

9 8 7 6 5 4 3 2 1
First Paperback Edition
Printed in the United States of America

♾This edition is printed on acid-free paper that meets the American National Standards Institute Z39.48 Standard.
♻ Shambhala Publications makes every effort to print on recycled paper. For more information please visit www.shambhala.com.

Distributed in the United States by Penguin Random House LLC and in Canada by Random House of Canada Ltd

Designed by Daniel Urban-Brown

Library of Congress catalogues the hardcover edition of this book as follows:
Names: Waldman, Sarah, author. | Cecil, Elizabeth, photographer.
Title: Feeding a family: a real-life plan for making dinner work / Sarah Waldman; photographs by Elizabeth Cecil.
Description: First edition. | Boulder: Roost Books, an imprint of Shambhala Publications, Inc., [2017] | Includes index.
Identifiers: LCCN 2016012234 | ISBN 9781611803099 (hardcover: alk. paper) | ISBN 9781611807431 (paperback: alk. paper)
Subjects: LCSH: Cooking, American. | Seasonal cooking. | Dinners and dining. | LCGFT: Cookbooks.
Classification: LCC TX715 .W176 2017 | DDC 641.5973—dc23 LC record available at https://lccn.loc.gov/2016012234

for Dylan & Gray—the loves of my life

Contents

Introduction

In the summer of 2008, I became obsessed with food. Not only food, but what was happening to food in America (spoiler alert—it wasn't and still isn't good). I read books by Marion Nestle, Michael Pollan, Mark Bittman, Sally Fallon, Walter Willett, and Ellyn Satter. I felt equally depressed and enlightened. Processed and packaged foods were trying to take over our country, and I became determined to help stop the epidemic of low-quality food appearing on family dinner tables.

I enrolled in the Institute of Integrative Nutrition, had a baby, then another, and began counseling people on how to navigate the modern food industry by building a diet made up of whole, seasonal foods. Today, as a busy mom of two young boys, my life still revolves around food, but in a completely different way. My reality is a hungry family that depends on me (mostly) to provide them with nutritious, home-cooked meals. And guess what—it's hard! Between work, school, and life I continually have to dig *really* deep to figure out how to pull this dinner thing off, night after night. My challenges are that one kid will devour a hamburger at twelve months while the other does not eat meat, we live nowhere near a big fancy grocery store, and we have a tight food budget.

The struggle to feed a family is real, and I know I'm not alone. Daily, friends will rush up to me in the school parking lot or library and ask, "What's for dinner?" They ask not because I'm an expert but because I might have an idea for something new, or I might just tell them it's okay to make egg sandwiches. Everyone wants to know how to make dinner work because when it works it is a great source of pride, connection, and light at the end of a long day. But when it doesn't work, dinnertime is depleting, depressing, and so unbelievably stressful.

But here's the thing—we shouldn't add cooking guilt to our already full plate of parental self-blame, especially when feeding our family is such a personal and emotional job. No matter who you are or what your cooking background may be, you can make the time for simple home-cooked dinners. You *can* reclaim dinner for your family.

I'm here to help with this daunting process. Throughout this book I offer guidance, inspiration, and concrete ideas on how to make family dinner work. And there is the food, of course. The recipes included in this book are our family favorites—the meals that have been in our regular rotation for years, as well as recent discoveries that have quickly become staples at our house. There are many recipes in this book that my kids eat weekly, if not daily, like Banana Milk with Flax Seeds (page 43) and Black Bean Quinoa Burgers (page 52). Other dishes that my husband, Nick, or I happen to love (hello, Roasted Green Beans with Scallions, page 206) are entirely aspirational: the boys have never chosen to eat a full bite of them, but I continue to cook and serve these foods, knowing that someday they may catch on.

Each season offers ten dinner menus. Some dinners are one-pot meals, while others have a few sides or even a dessert. I hope the menu-style organization takes the guesswork out of what to serve with what and gives you a good list to start with at the beginning of each season. Although many dinners have desserts, I am not suggesting you make and eat dessert this often. Rather, I'm hoping these simple, wholesome sweets will come in handy when planning a seasonal celebration, special birthday treat (let's try not to bring loads of artificial sugar into schools), or after-school baking project (sanity saved!).

These recipes are for easy, everyday meals, but many of the dinners can be simplified and adapted even further. For example, Creamy Pumpkin Fettuccine (page 73), which calls for spinach fettuccine to be tossed in creamy pumpkin alfredo sauce and then topped with pumpkin seed pesto, is still delicious with just one sauce—creamy or pesto. And Sweet Pea Oven Risotto (page 104) is great with finely chopped asparagus instead of peas. Make the recipes your own by subbing in your family's favorite ingredients and the produce available around your home. Each season also offers a slower Sunday dinner that often involves family participation. These are the kinds of meals that start in the morning, chug along, and end with a messy kitchen and full table.

I have invited four guest families to share their favorite seasonal dinners so you can see what works in other family kitchens. These families are all busy, hardworking, down-to-earth food lovers. You'll also notice that I've included notes throughout the book on how to adapt the dinners to feed an infant (nobody wants to unnecessarily cook the baby a separate meal), recipe tasks kids can do, and ways to transform parts of the meal into a second dinner.

We started documenting our family meals for this book in the winter, so that is where the recipes start. All the cooking, photography, and writing were completed in season, thus the stories and recipes take us through one full year, in real time.

How to Feed a Family

So how exactly do we pull this nightly family dinner thing off—not just getting a meal on the table but actually enjoying it? This section explores the big ideas behind the family meal, from why family dinner is so important to what can be done about "picky eaters." Here, I have outlined my personal inspirations, ideas, and steps for creating a rhythm of home-cooked dinners. These thoughts are organized into bulleted, easy-to-read lists so your precious time is not wasted searching for helpful bits amid lengthy paragraphs. I hope you find nuggets of information here that really resonate with you. I drafted these lists to be photocopied and hung on a fridge, e-mailed between friends, or used to kick off an important family meeting. I still reference many of these reminders on a daily basis and hope that you leave this section energized and inspired.

THE BENEFITS OF FAMILY DINNER

At our core we all know family dinners are a good idea. Maybe it's the memory of a meal decades ago—one where you heard an infamous family story for the first time or watched your infant try, and love, curry chicken. Perhaps it was the meal when you noticed your twelve-year-old son looking like a teenager. Strong memories and emotions are good reasons to eat together, but the facts don't hurt either.

Children embrace the predictability of a nightly family event.

Dinner conversations support and expand children's verbal and reading skills.

Family dinner time is a rare opportunity to share family history and stories.

(continued)

At mealtime, parents and older children model expected social behavior, which helps younger children develop their own social skills.

It is generally agreed that children who eat with parents or siblings at the table eat more nutritious foods during their meal.

Children who participate in regular family meals do better nutritionally, academically, socially, and emotionally. (Ellyn Satter, *Secrets of Feeding a Healthy Family*)

Regular family meals affect children more positively than extracurricular activities, church, tutoring, and music lessons do. (Ellyn Satter, *Secrets of Feeding a Healthy Family*)

Teenagers who eat dinner with their families are less likely to smoke, drink alcohol, and do drugs. (The National Center on Addiction & Substance Abuse at Columbia University)

FAMILY NUTRITION AND SEASONAL WHOLE FOODS

Nutrition information is overwhelming and often confusing. We are bombarded with nutritional messages everywhere, from food packaging (Fiber! No sugar!) to articles in parenting magazines (Try this new superfood!) and meaningful conversations with our pediatricians. Often, the language is hard to understand and the different messages quickly contradict each other. I think we have overcomplicated things. My advice is to simply focus on eating and serving a variety of whole foods—that's it. If the food is in season, cue the fireworks.

Cooking and eating what is growing outside is not a new concept, but the availability of global produce has made us numb to the natural connection between season and plant. Children, however, are naturally aware of the changing seasons (imagine a five-year-old on the first snowy day), and we can take a cue from them. By building our meals with what is growing, we automatically satisfy our cravings and consume foods that our bodies need (think nutrient-dense sweet potatoes in the winter and hydrating melons in the summer). I realize that there are so many rules around eating healthfully, seasonally, and locally that a very simple and natural process has become overly confusing, daunting, and not so fun. I encourage you to ease up on expectations and guilt. Just being aware of what is in season and doing your best to work some of those items into your family's meals is enough. You can always build upon your initial efforts. And remember, nobody is perfect. We treat our boys to blueberry-topped yogurt in February and buy bananas that grow far away from our northern home. In the end, I think a bowl full of blueberries is still better than none—if those berries are from your local farmer or garden, all the better.

It is important to note that every body is different—some people feel their best eating dairy, red meat, or wheat, while others have adverse reactions to these foods. No two bodies need and want the exact same things. Above all else, I hope this information will allow you to step back and look at the big picture.

Before you serve it, ask: *Is this a whole food?* Meaning, can a farmer grow it? Is it a whole or piece of an original food? For example, an apple is whole, but apple juice is not. How long have people been planting, eating, and cooking this food? Generally, the more unprocessed a food is, the more nutrients it contains.

Adults and children should eat a balanced diet made up of whole grains, vegetables, proteins (legumes, nuts, seeds, dairy, meat, poultry, fish, eggs, tofu), fruits, and fats (nuts, seeds, avocado, oils, coconut, lard). Everybody finds his or her own balance between these foods. Use these groups to guide your daily, weekly, and monthly meal planning. You can also use this as a tool for kids to choose the components of meals (just pick a favorite item from a few categories). A quick review of these general categories makes it clear what types of foods your family, child, or self are lacking. In the end, step back and ask yourself: *Did our family meet these requirements over a meal, week, month, or season?*

No one food group has all the nutrients our bodies need, but all the basic food groups combined offer a nutritious diet.

Nutrition directly affects daily energy, mood, temperament, and long-term health for adults and children alike.

Your family's eating attitudes and relationships with food are more important than what they actually eat on any given day. If general attitudes and behaviors are positive, individuals will eat well and get the nutrition they need.

(continued)

Rather than labeling a food as "not bad" (for example, you may think crackers are "not bad" compared to a donut), ask yourself: *What is the nutritional benefit of this food?* This question helps me clarify and focus on foods that have a positive effect on the health of my family and me, and separate out those that are not obviously harmful but do not offer important nutritional benefits either (like those crackers).

When you do order a pizza (or another favorite takeout dinner) after a marathon day, serve it with a bowl of raw, sliced fruit and vegetables and your family's favorite milk or smoothie. This way, everyone will fill up on a variety of foods and not overdo it on takeout.

Locally grown food tastes better, as it is not packed and shipped far distances or picked before it's ripe. It also produces less pollution, due to its short travel time.

Shopping locally keeps your money in your local economy.

When you see a price tag, think of what that food is also "costing" in terms of your health, environment, and the local economy.

Join a CSA (community-supported agriculture) or plant a garden for access to high-quality produce. If a child grows a plant, they are more likely to taste and enjoy it.

Freeze in-season produce for use year-round. Cleaned and chopped produce is best frozen on large baking sheets, then transferred to freezer bags to eliminate big clumps.

Buying in bulk means that you are not spending your money on unnecessary packaging and advertising.

Encourage your favorite and most conveniently located markets to offer more locally grown items.

Find a balance between your budget and your ideals.

Time is the biggest obstacle to the family dinner. But, feeding your family is *really* important, and, I dare say, feeding your family poorly can become dangerous. Adjust your priorities to make the time to prepare a handful of planned dinners every week (maybe three or four), and fill out the rest of the week with quick pantry meals (see page 14).

First, look at your activities and then do some time juggling. What does your family's extracurricular time look like over the week or month? How much is spent on things like baseball practice vs. cooking for yourselves? Block off time on the weekends, early mornings, or evenings, or outsource specific tasks to your partner. Too tired to cook after work? Then don't cook after work! Maybe it is as simple as getting up twenty minutes earlier to get dinner into the slow cooker, moving a radio into the kitchen, or watching your favorite show while prepping on Sunday. No one is asking you to give up things you like, but feeding a family does take thought and time. We need to make meal planning, shopping, and prepping a priority. Our modern culture is trying to convince us that time spent on dinner preparation is wasted time, and that we need to multitask during mealtime to keep up. Not true. What we need is to find ways to make cooking food and eating together fit into our busy lives. It is not a lost cause, but it does require a unified effort.

Aim to cook three or four dinners a week. Fill out the rest of the week with quick pantry dinners (page 14) or leftovers.

Plan your weekly meals as a family by looking through cookbooks and magazines or reviewing a small notebook of favorite recorded meals.

Build and maintain a well-stocked pantry (more on this on page 13). You'll always pick up more groceries than you really need at the store (even with a good list), but if you know your kitchen is full of useful ingredients at all times, you'll be less likely to overbuy.

Clean out the pantry and fridge as often as you can, and while you put weekly groceries away, consolidate containers of the same item, recycle empty containers, toss what is old, and organize the rest.

(continued)

Once a month, shop for pantry items and staples. Once a week, shop for produce. Keep an ongoing shopping list on the fridge organized into two columns: pantry and produce.

All family members can help with supporting jobs, such as quickly organizing the pantry and fridge during grocery unpacking, adding items to a master shopping list, loading and unloading the dishwasher, setting and clearing the table, and emptying the garbage.

Prepping even the smallest thing ahead of time helps—mixing a sauce, filling a pot with water, or arranging vegetables on a roasting tray.

Prepare produce whenever you can before cooking time. Chopping onions, peeling carrots, and washing kale leaves seem like small steps but are a huge help come cooking time.

Cook ahead. Preparing a pot of whole grains, a tray of roasted vegetables, or side dishes that can keep in the fridge makes mealtime all the more organized.

Use some canned and packaged foods. Things like canned beans, whole peeled tomatoes, and low-sodium chicken broth are no-brainers in a busy kitchen.

Invest in machines that help. A basic food processor, blender, and grill pan are all simple time-saving tools in a family kitchen.

Look to your equally busy friends for support. Maybe you gather on Sunday afternoons to cook or shop together. You can also each make a batch of something (pizza dough, soup) and trade to share the wealth.

INVOLVING THE WHOLE FAMILY

The goal is to avoid placing the brunt of family dinner responsibilities (from meal brainstorming to shopping, prepping, cooking, and cleaning) on just one person. If these important roles fall to one family member, that person is going to get burnt out, resentful, or just stop having fun. We are looking for a long-term solution that is sustainable and inclusive of all family members. Dinnertime will be the most successful if everyone takes some ownership and draws pride from the process. And in the long run, what is the worst that could happen by inviting the kids to crack a few eggs or chop the celery? Sure, you may have to choke down a couple of eggshell bites or serve a very "rustic"-looking salad, but there will be no long-term damages.

Hold a family meeting to kick off your dinner project. Talk about why it is going to be so fun and have family members choose jobs, such as recipe selection, shopping help, table setting, picking flowers for the table, calling the family to dinner, making homemade placemats or nametags, and cleaning up by carrying dishes to the sink, sweeping the floor, and loading the dishwasher.

Always invite the kids to help with cooking, but if they don't want to, don't push it.

Follow your children's lead in the kitchen—see what they like to cook and what tasks interest them. Maybe physical work like tearing kale leaves and peeling or chopping vegetables is their thing. Calmer tasks like measuring and mixing or decorating the dinner table appeal to others.

Invest in child-friendly kitchen tools that work for your kids. Tools that are unsafe or frustrating make cooking together stressful. (Hello, nervous hovering parent!) Our boys' favorite kitchen tools are a pizza cutter (to slice bread, tortillas, greens, soft fruit), child-safe knives (for general chopping and slicing), kitchen shears (for trimming fruits and vegetables), and small wooden rolling pins and mixing spoons. We also have a light-but-sturdy kitchen stool, which the boys can move around themselves when they need a boost.

Lead by example. If you are angry and frazzled in the kitchen, it is likely everyone in the house is going to pick up on your feelings. Sad but true. It is best to invite younger kids to help when you are in a good mood and not in a total rush.

Relax. Cooking with little people (or your partner!) is not always smooth sailing. Things spill, more baking powder is added than you had hoped, some of the sliced apples are huge (with seeds hanging off) and others are tiny slivers. This is what family dinner looks like, and it is okay. Overly correcting and imposing rules on kitchen helpers is going to lower their pride and discourage them from helping next time. And yes, your kitchen is going to get messy.

FEEDING KIDS AND "PICKY EATERS"

"Picky eaters" is a new phrase that did not exist in our grandparents' time. By picky eaters I am not talking about those who have confirmed food allergies or medical sensitivities; I am talking about kids who can (seemingly) not participate in family meals. I completely understand why and how picky eating habits are formed, because we as busy parents ease up on the expectations of our children's eating. We are exhausted, frustrated, and feel guilty about almost everything. At the start, however, most babies are enthusiastic eaters. In fact, infants often show a pure, open relationship with food. As kids grow up, behaviors, personalities, and opinions are thrown into the mix and things get complicated. The truth is, kids are capable of eating a range of whole foods, and we as parents can be sensitive to their likes and dislikes without catering to every request. Believe it or not, the pressure to eat a variety of whole foods is already within your child—in their desire to grow and to mirror you as a grown-up. The meals your family cooks and serves will become a fact of your child's world, and they will adapt to dinnertime like they do to everything else. It's the period of adaptation that is bumpy.

When I needed help with a picky preschooler, I turned to Ellyn Satter, a family therapist, feeding expert, and the author of a collection of books about nutrition and feeding of children. I found Satter's advice extremely helpful when our oldest son was four and our youngest was one. I was exhausted and had slacked off on our family's eating habits. With renewed determination and energy, we regrouped and dramatically improved our family meals. The following advice is gleaned from Satter's various books and writings, and has helped me and my family stay on track and deal with the issue of pickiness.

Hold a family meeting to discuss the start of new dinner rules or to regroup after noticing changes at mealtime. I find myself calling a family dinner meeting every few months to remind our family of our basic rules.

Phones and other electronic devices are not allowed at the table for any family members.

Arrange food choices on the table and let everyone pick what they like. It's okay if someone chooses only one food, but there should be at least one food item that you know everyone likes. More often than not, our dinnertime spread includes a loaf of whole-wheat bread with butter and a bowl of sliced apples.

Find meals that can be tweaked with toppings or sauces to meet individual preferences, like Kale and Sweet Potato Tacos (page 78) and Noodle Bowls (page 26).

Avoid meals made up of all new ingredients. Children like to see something familiar.

Nobody should be pressured into eating anything they don't like, provided that they say "no, thank you" politely (not "yuck!"). Family members (including adults) can say "that's not my style" or "I don't like the tomatoes" (or other specific ingredient) so it is clear what is a turnoff. It is okay to spit something out after you try it.

Try not to stress out if specific foods are refused (for example, leafy greens or brown rice). Focus on eating those items yourself and offer them again at another meal.

Stay cool. Do your best not to comment on your kids' eating at the dinner table. Serve the food, then watch what people choose, eat, and decline without fanfare.

The kitchen is closed after dinner. If kids choose not to eat dinner, no biggie—they just have to wait until the next meal. Yes, this can be extremely hard in the beginning (I've been in many a "just a banana!!!" life-or-death situations), but if you are consistent and dinner happens at roughly the same time every night, kids will know what to expect and the consequences that come with their choices.

Babies, toddlers, and children can take a long time to eat, as the event is as much about filling their bellies as it is about exploring colors and textures, practicing feeding, and using utensils. Don't rush through dinner; rather, sit tight and go at their pace.

Take care in what you (and other role models) eat, as children are observing you and are very influenced by your choices. Think about your relationship with the "picky" foods. Do you cook, serve, and eat a lot of them?

(continued)

Look at what time you're eating dinner. I slowly discovered (after watching trays and trays of snacks being gobbled up) that our boys are the most hungry and truly ready to eat dinner at 4:30 or 5:00 P.M. each day. This makes sense, as they are home from a long day and are asleep just a couple of hours later. Of course, it is a challenge to have a family meal at this time, but the earlier you serve dinner, the less snacking is necessary and the more hunger (a natural motivator) will kick-start mealtime eating.

Keep perspective. When Gray was an infant, I was really worried that he was eating too many bananas. He wanted a banana with every meal, so naturally I thought I did something wrong and he would never eat foods without a sweet fruit included. I came to realize that if my biggest feeding problem was that my baby really liked bananas, then I had it good. He outgrew the banana phase pretty quickly.

Don't camouflage the "picky" food in a recipe, but instead include it with a favorite food. Hiding healthy foods makes children distrustful and suspicious. I'd rather have my kids know what broccoli looks and tastes like, and not like it, than try to hide the vegetable from them in pancakes and brownies. However, serving something like broccoli in a favorite food (pasta, rice, or soup) is one way to open them up to the food in a familiar way.

If it's not on their plate (or on your dinner table), they can't eat it. I realize how ridiculous this sounds, but it's true. The only way kids can get used to a new food and have the opportunity to try it again is if it is served to them—again and again.

If dessert is a struggle (a bargaining tool, constant request, or nightly argument), start by not making it a reward. Instead, put a sensible serving of dessert at each place when you set the table. Dessert should not be served every night. Sometimes a simple dark chocolate chip is our "dessert," and it goes over very well. Ultimately, sweet treats that are no longer banned become normal foods that can be consumed in normal ways.

Keep Ellyn Satter's golden rule (from *Secrets of Feeding a Healthy Family*) in mind: "You do the feeding and your child does the eating and growing. Parents are responsible for what, when, where of feeding. Children are responsible for how much and whether of eating."

Building a Family Pantry

A well-stocked pantry is a key piece of the dinner puzzle. When staple items are stocked and organized, cooking dinner is faster and shopping trips are less daunting (not to mention that feeling of triumph when I open the pantry to look for a specific ingredient and find it there staring at me!). On those nights when you come home late or don't have a specific dinner planned, a simple meal can be quickly prepared from a well-stocked pantry.

MY PANTRY STAPLES

This master list includes every pantry item you need to cook every dish in this book. I find all these items in our small town market and keep them in my kitchen at all times.

DRIED FRUIT

Dates

Dried Peaches

Raisins

FLOURS

Bread Flour

Buckwheat Flour

Cornmeal

Unbleached All-Purpose Flour

Whole-Wheat All-Purpose Flour

Whole-Wheat Pastry Flour

LEGUMES

Black Beans

Chickpeas

Green Lentils

Red Lentils

MISCELLANEOUS

Arrowroot Powder

Bread Crumbs (panko and regular)

Chicken Broth

Coconut Milk

Diced Tomatoes

Dijon Mustard

(cont.)

Hot Sauce

Miso Paste

Nori

Sriracha

Tomato Paste

Unsweetened Cocoa Powder

Unsweetened Shredded Coconut

Vegetable Broth

Whole Peeled Tomatoes

Worcestershire Sauce

NUTS AND SEEDS

- Almond Butter
- Almonds (sliced and whole)
- Chia Seeds
- Flax Seeds
- Hazelnuts
- Peanuts (dry roasted)
- Peanut Butter
- Pecans
- Pine Nuts
- Pumpkin Seeds (Pepitas)
- Sesame Seeds
- Tahini

OILS

- Canola Oil
- Coconut Oil
- Extra Virgin Olive Oil
- Sesame Oil

PASTAS AND NOODLES

- Dried Semolina Pasta
- Dried Spinach Pasta

(cont.)

- Dried Whole-Wheat Pasta
- Soba Noodles
- Udon Noodles

SPICES AND FLAVORINGS

- Chili Powder
- Cinnamon (ground)
- Cumin (ground)
- Curry Paste
- Curry Powder
- Pure Vanilla Extract
- Red Pepper Flakes
- Turmeric (ground)

SWEETENERS

- Agave Nectar
- Brown Rice Syrup
- Brown Sugar
- Cane Sugar
- Coconut Sugar
- Honey
- Maple Syrup (pure)

VINEGARS

- Apple Cider Vinegar
- Red Wine Vinegar
- Rice Vinegar

WHOLE GRAINS

- Arborio Rice
- Barley
- Black Forbidden Rice
- Brown Rice
- Farro
- Long-Grain Rice
- Quinoa
- Red Bulgur
- Sushi Rice

QUICK DINNERS FROM PANTRY AND FRIDGE STAPLES

Remember, dinner does not have to be a life-changing meal every night. Here are our favorite dinners made from pantry and fridge staples. Some of these ideas may not look like "dinner" to you, but I would like to redefine the term. To me, any home-cooked meal—however simple—is a successful dinner.

ROASTED VEGGIE PASTA: Toss cooked pasta with roasted vegetables and tomato sauce or pesto.

BAKED SWEET POTATO BAR: Serve baked sweet potatoes with refried beans, cheese, and other toppings on the side.

EGG SANDWICHES: Layer fried eggs, sliced avocado, tomato, red onion, and cheese on toasted bread.

RICE & BEANS: Cook a pot of rice, stir in a can of drained and rinsed beans, and serve with toppings such as sliced mango, cabbage slaw, ground pork, sour cream, or cheese.

FRUITY BUTTERMILK PANCAKES: Make buttermilk pancake batter and dot with fresh, seasonal fruit before cooking.

PANTRY SOUP: In a large pot, combine a quart or two of chicken stock, drained chickpeas, baby spinach leaves, fresh lemon juice, and leftover rice, tortellini, or shredded chicken. Heat until warm.

KIDNEY BEAN DIP: In a food processor, puree two cans of drained kidney beans with two cups of shredded jack cheese and some pickled jalapeños (to taste). Scoop the dip into a casserole dish and warm it in the oven; serve with pita chips and cut veggies.

GREEN BREAKFAST: Scramble some eggs, stir in finely chopped sautéed greens, and serve with roasted potatoes and bacon.

SAUSAGES & PEPPERS: Grill up local sausages and top them with a quick sauté of colorful peppers and onions. Serve with whatever grain you want to use up.

TACOS OR BURRITOS: Fill small corn or flour tortillas with almost anything, from grilled chicken and avocado to refried beans and scrambled eggs.

SOBA NOODLES & TOFU: Boil soba noodles and toss them with low-sodium soy sauce and sesame oil. In a hot, oiled pan, stir-fry cubed tofu and any vegetables you have on hand. Add the noodles to the pan and toss well.

PARFAITS: In tall glasses, layer whole-milk yogurt, homemade granola, and fresh berries.

QUICK CURRY: Stir a couple of tablespoons of curry paste into a can of full-fat coconut milk. Squirt in some lemon, thin it out with water, and toss in drained chickpeas or leftover chicken—maybe even some frozen peas. Simmer over medium heat until warmed through. Serve with brown rice.

Winter

Winter dinners do so much. They warm us up physically, from the snow and wind, and mentally, from the idea of *five months* of snow and wind. Fierce winter storms often cause the ferries to and from Martha's Vineyard to stop running, and suddenly we find ourselves stranded on an island, or perhaps even stranded inside a small cottage, for days upon end. Desperate times call for desperate measures—another Chocolate, Peanut Butter, and Date Truffle (page 29), anyone? Despite the challenges, winter may be my favorite cooking season. It is about hunkering down, making do with what you have, and eating filling meals before heading off early to bed. The dark afternoons and evenings are long, so it is the perfect time to focus on family participation in the kitchen, whether that involves looking through a cookbook to pick out a new soup or rolling sushi together for a Roasted Root Vegetable Sushi Bar (page 38). But perhaps most important, winter meals soothe sick bodies, tired and weak with runny noses. Working a variety of winter greens, hot broths, and vitamin C–packed citrus into your family's cold-weather diet will help ward off some of the ickiness. Happily, our hardy winter dinners lend themselves to leftovers that taste even better the next day, packed into lunch boxes or transformed into second meals.

Winter Meals

Pizza Night

KALE, HERBED RICOTTA, AND LOCAL SAUSAGE PAN PIZZA

FRESH CITRUS FRUIT

Our oldest son has never eaten a piece of animal meat. This is going on five-plus years, and I'm curious to see where it ends up. His brother, on the other hand, dove for a spicy pork taco and gobbled it down in a flash just after his first birthday. Needless to say, they have different tastes. Pizza is one of those simple family dinners that pleases us all. We often top half the pie with something most of the family likes and the other half with another thing most of the family likes—I call that even. Don't let this pizza dough intimidate you. It's something you can throw together the night before and leave until dinnertime the next evening. To balance out the hearty pizza, I often slice up a few citrus fruits for a refreshing and simple side. Anything from clementines to blood oranges or grapefruits will do—they all add welcomed winter freshness to our table.

KALE, HERBED RICOTTA, AND LOCAL SAUSAGE PAN PIZZA

makes one 12 by 18-inch pan pizza

Over the past nine years, Nick has been on a quest to master a variety of pizza techniques at home, from a classic Margherita to this "Grandma" pie. He has experimented with different flour varieties, forms of tomato (fresh, canned, sauce), cheeses, and cooking techniques. Happily, his hard work has led us to some darn good home-cooked pizza. If you're feeding a crowd (or love cold pizza as much as we do), simply make two bowls of dough and put the kids in charge of their own pie to have ready for lunch boxes the next day. In the cold months, this dense pan pizza is our favorite. Here, a simple overnight dough (just mix and leave it in the fridge before bed) is topped with creamy ricotta cheese, pork sausage, and kale. As an added bonus, the 500°F oven is a welcome guest in a cold, February kitchen, always taking the edge off the drafts coming up through the floorboards.

KIDS CAN: Little helpers can tear kale leaves from stems, stir the ricotta cheese mixture, and push the pizza dough into the pan.

DOUGH

1 package (2¼ teaspoons) active dry yeast

1½ cups warm water

1 teaspoon kosher salt

3 tablespoons extra virgin olive oil, divided

4 cups unbleached all-purpose flour

PIZZA

1 big bunch kale (about 13 kale leaves)

5 tablespoons extra virgin olive oil, divided

¼ cup water

Kosher salt

1 pound pork sausage (hot or sweet), removed from casings

1 cup whole-milk ricotta cheese

Zest of ½ lemon

Leaves from 2 sprigs fresh thyme, chopped

Leaves from 1 sprig fresh rosemary, chopped

1 cup marinara sauce (your favorite brand or homemade)

---

1. Make the dough the night before your pizza dinner. First, in a large bowl, whisk the yeast into the water until it dissolves. Let the mix stand for 10 minutes (you should see some bubbly foam form on top of the water). Using a wooden spoon, stir in the salt and 2 tablespoons of the olive oil, then add the flour 1 cup at a time, stirring after each addition. Mix everything together and turn the dough out onto a floured countertop. Knead for 5 minutes until

soft and springy. Place the kneaded dough into a clean bowl coated with the remaining tablespoon of olive oil. Cover the bowl with plastic wrap and leave it in the fridge until dinnertime the following day.

2. Take the dough out of the fridge to come to room temperature. When you're ready to make the pizza, set a rack in the lower third of your oven and preheat to 500°F. While the oven heats, slice the kale leaves into thin ribbons. Heat 2 tablespoons of the olive oil in a large skillet over medium heat, add the kale ribbons, water, and a pinch of salt, and sauté for 5 minutes, until the kale is wilted. Transfer the kale to a plate and use the same pan to cook the sausage. Cook the sausage over medium heat until brown, about 10 minutes, breaking the meat apart with the back of a wooden spoon.

3. While the kale and sausage cook, mix the ricotta in a small bowl with a pinch of salt, the lemon zest, and the chopped thyme and rosemary.

4. To prepare for baking, coat a 12 by 18-inch rimmed baking sheet with the remaining 3 tablespoons of olive oil. Slowly stretch the dough across the pan, pushing it into the corners with your fingers. Top the dough with a layer of tomato sauce, then add the kale, sausage, and small dollops of the flavored ricotta. Bake for 15 minutes. Remove the pizza from the oven, cut it into squares, and serve immediately.

FOR BABY: Finely chop a bit of cooked sausage and kale, then mix it with ¼ cup of plain ricotta cheese. Thin out the mixture with water or milk if it looks too dry. Finely dice some citrus fruits for finger food.

Slurpee Noodle Bowls

NOODLE BOWLS

CHOCOLATE, PEANUT BUTTER, AND DATE TRUFFLES

Like most kids I know, Dylan counts peanut noodles among his favorite meals. After serving up my hundredth batch of peanut noodles, I knew we had to shake things up—at least for my own sake! This meal is inspired by the creamy and salty noodles we all love but with fresh, crisp toppings and a warming broth. After a light meal like Noodle Bowls, one of us will almost always request something rich and sweet for dessert. As this request typically falls right before bedtime, a labor-intensive baking project is not in the cards. However, quick Chocolate, Peanut Butter, and Date Truffles can be made in under ten minutes. The slightly sticky, chocolate-scented dough is ideal for little hands to roll and decorate, creating the perfect, nutritious treat to nibble on with a bedtime story or while being coaxed into a warm bath.

NOODLE BOWLS

serves 4

Don't be turned off by the long list of ingredients—this dinner is really just a dash of this and spritz of that all piled into one simple pot. If your family is not a fan of tofu, simply omit it or replace it with your favorite vegetables or shredded meat. Regular pasta is also a fine replacement for udon noodles if you don't have them on hand.

KIDS CAN: Put older kids in charge of preparing the noodle bowl toppings.

NOODLE BOWLS

2 garlic cloves

1 yellow onion

1-inch piece fresh gingerroot

2 tablespoons canola oil, divided

1 to 2 tablespoons green curry paste

1 teaspoon agave nectar

1 teaspoon sesame oil

½ teaspoon kosher salt

1 teaspoon ground turmeric

5 tablespoons soy sauce

1 package extra-firm tofu, cut into ¼-inch cubes

One 15-ounce can full-fat coconut milk

3 cups chicken broth

8 ounces udon noodles

Juice of 1 lime

1 tablespoon creamy peanut butter

TOPPINGS

1 shallot, minced

½ head purple cabbage, finely shredded

1 lime, sliced

1 cup dry roasted peanuts, chopped

1 cup bean sprouts

1 cup chopped fresh cilantro

Sriracha

1. Using a food processor, whiz the garlic, onion, and ginger together until finely minced. In a medium soup pot, heat 1 tablespoon of the canola oil over medium heat. Add the garlic, onion, and ginger mixture and cook until soft and fragrant, about 3 minutes. Add in the curry paste, agave, sesame oil, salt, turmeric, and soy sauce and cook for another 3 minutes, stirring everything together. Add in the tofu and gently toss the cubes to coat them with the flavored mixture. Next, pour in the coconut milk and broth. Bring the soup to a strong simmer, then turn the heat down to low and let it cook while you prepare the noodles and toppings.
2. Cook the noodles per the package directions (typically 6 minutes in boiling water). Strain the noodles and toss them with the remaining tablespoon of canola oil.
3. Depending on your time, prepare the toppings by hand or use a food processor to shred the cabbage and finely chop the shallot, peanuts, and cilantro in quick batches.
4. Before serving, finish the broth by whisking in the lime juice and peanut butter. Taste the

broth and add more curry paste or soy sauce if need be. To serve, pile the noodles in the bottom of individual soup bowls, top with broth, and then pile on the toppings.

FOR BABY: In a small saucepan, warm a handful of minced tofu and cooked noodles in ½ cup of plain chicken broth.

TOMORROW'S DINNER: STIR-FRY

Shred the remaining half head of purple cabbage and, using a large wok, stir-fry the cabbage, some thinly sliced chicken/pork/tofu, garlic, and fresh ginger in canola oil. Serve over brown rice with any remaining noodle bowl toppings.

CHOCOLATE, PEANUT BUTTER, AND DATE TRUFFLES

makes 20 truffles

Not only are these raw truffles the perfect treat before an early January bedtime, but they also make ideal Valentine's Day "candies" for school friends, teachers, or neighbors. Tailor the recipe for your valentine by choosing a favorite food (salty peanuts in this case) to coat the balls with—anything from toasted shredded coconut to crystallized ginger works. If you're feeling extra ambitious (or have a long, dark afternoon on your hands), make a variety pack with a few different toppings.

KIDS CAN: For some sticky fun, kids can be in charge of pitting the dates and rolling the truffles.

- 2 lightly packed cups pitted dates
- ½ teaspoon pure vanilla extract
- ⅓ cup creamy peanut butter
- ¼ cup unsweetened shredded coconut
- 2 tablespoons natural cocoa powder
- Pinch of kosher salt
- ⅓ cup dry roasted peanuts, chopped

---

1. Using a food processor, whiz the dates and vanilla together until a sticky paste forms. Add in the peanut butter, coconut, cocoa powder, and salt. Pulse about a dozen times to combine all the ingredients.
2. When you're ready to roll the truffles, put the chopped peanuts in a shallow bowl and turn the truffle dough out onto a clean counter. Using your hands, grab a golf ball–size piece of dough and roll it into a ball. Place the ball into the peanuts and gently roll it around to adhere the nuts. Continue rolling out all the truffles. The finished truffles can be stored in an airtight container at room temperature for a few days, or in the refrigerator for up to 2 weeks. They are best served at room temperature.

FOR BABY: Finely chop a couple of dates and roll the sticky pieces in a sprinkling of coconut.

The One-Skillet Wonders

CHICKEN THIGHS WITH BARLEY, CHARD, AND MUSHROOMS

CINNAMON AND SUGAR CHICKPEAS

Who doesn't love a dinner that involves just tossing everything into one pan? It makes preparing dinner a cinch, and won't add more pots and pans to the already aggressive pile of sink dishes. Often times one-pot meals (I'm thinking women's magazine casseroles here) call for too many cans of processed ingredients, filled with sodium and additives, to be mixed together into an unidentifiable mush. Not here—in this dish, whole grains, leafy greens, tomatoes, and chicken are layered together and popped into the oven. If you have time in the evening, early morning, or during naptime, this skillet can be assembled in five minutes, covered, and left in the fridge, waiting for you. Now go put that time saved on dishes to some good use (with a warming whisky cocktail, perhaps?).

CHICKEN THIGHS WITH BARLEY, CHARD, AND MUSHROOMS

serves 4

When I first came up with this simple one-skillet dinner, I shared it with my sister Anna, knowing it was right up her alley. Later that day, she sent me a picture of her cast iron skillet meal, along with a note: "Toss in a cup of barley with the veggies—it's great." Genius! The liquid from the veggies and chicken plumps up the barley beautifully, and in just forty minutes you have a complete meal ready to go. If mushrooms aren't your thing, or if you are throwing this together in the summer, use halved cherry tomatoes or thinly sliced zucchini rounds instead—both work perfectly.

---

3 tablespoons olive oil, divided
One 28-ounce can diced tomatoes
1 bunch Swiss chard, leaves removed from stems and torn into small pieces (stems can be saved for soup or stir-fry)
8 ounces white button mushrooms, stemmed and chopped
2 garlic cloves, smashed
2 teaspoons kosher salt, plus more as needed
1 cup barley
1 cup low-sodium chicken broth
4 bone-in, skin-on chicken thighs
Freshly ground black pepper
4 sprigs fresh thyme
1 lemon, sliced

---

1. Preheat the oven to 425°F. Brush 2 tablespoons of the olive oil across the bottom of a 10-inch cast iron skillet. In a large bowl, toss together the tomatoes, chard, mushrooms, garlic, and 1 teaspoon of the salt. Place half of the vegetable mixture in the bottom of the cast iron skillet, and pour the barley over the top. Add the rest of the vegetable mixture and the chicken broth.

2. Arrange the chicken thighs on top of the veggie and barley layers, pushing them gently into the skillet. Sprinkle the chicken with the remaining teaspoon of salt and a few grinds of pepper, then drizzle the skins with the remaining tablespoon of olive oil. Toss in the thyme and sliced lemon. Transfer the skillet to the oven and roast for 35 to 45 minutes until the skin begins to brown and the barley is tender. If you like extra-crisp skin, put the pan under the broiler for the last few minutes. Serve immediately.

FOR BABY: Mash a small bowl of chicken, barley, and vegetables with the back of a spoon or puree the mixture with an immersion blender.

TOMORROW'S DINNER: SOUP

Create a simple chicken, barley, and vegetable soup. Heat a small pot of chicken or vegetable broth and stir in any leftover diced chicken and vegetable-barley mixture. Simmer over low heat, just to warm it through. Serve with Parmesan cheese and crusty bread.

CINNAMON AND SUGAR CHICKPEAS

serves 4

The mild flavor and creamy texture of chickpeas allow these beans to be easily transformed into a high-protein treat. Here, I toss them with coconut oil, cinnamon, and sugar and sauté them until crisp and golden. Your house will smell as good as they taste.

---

19 ounces canned chickpeas
2 tablespoons coconut oil
Pinch of kosher salt
3 tablespoons granulated sweetener (coconut sugar, pure cane sugar, or date sugar)
2 teaspoons ground cinnamon

---

1. Drain and rinse the chickpeas, then dry them on a kitchen towel. If the skins pop off during the drying process, simply discard them.
2. Melt the coconut oil in a medium skillet over medium heat.
3. In a large mixing bowl, stir together the chickpeas, salt, granulated sweetener, cinnamon, and 1 tablespoon of the melted coconut oil (leave the remaining coconut oil in the skillet). Ask your little helper to stir until all the chickpeas are coated.
4. Turn the skillet up to medium-high heat. Toss in the flavored chickpeas and arrange them in a single layer. Let the chickpeas crisp up for about 2 minutes without stirring, then toss them and repeat the crisping/tossing process until they are caramelized and smell delicious, about 2 to 5 minutes more. Cinnamon and Sugar Chickpeas are best eaten warm right out of the pan.

FOR BABY: Smash a few crispy chickpeas with the back of a fork for finger feeding.

Japanese Takeout at Home

ROASTED ROOT VEGETABLE SUSHI BAR

QUICK MISO SOUP

BANANA MILK WITH FLAX SEEDS

I know it is the start of the long, dark season when I find myself turning the car's headlights on while driving home from school. When dinnertime rolls around, the sky is pitch-black and I feel like it could be midnight, despite the rambunctious kids playing nearby. These long evenings need a spark to keep my spirits up. When we lived in a city, the spark was a stroll down to our favorite Thai or Japanese restaurant, but these days that is not an option. Martha's Vineyard's winter food scene is far from diverse (you won't find pho or curry anywhere), so we have to do it ourselves. This sushi bar and miso soup dinner is our best attempt at making a takeout meal of our own. To top it off, I am sharing the boys' most loved one-minute dessert.

ROASTED ROOT VEGETABLE SUSHI BAR

makes 5 to 6 rolls

Meals that encourage family collaboration, like this Roasted Root Vegetable Sushi Bar, rolled along to a little music, help to keep me out of the winter dumps. Our sushi bar allows for family members to build what they like and take charge of their dinner.

P.S.: You only have to cook rice and roast a tray of vegetables!

KIDS CAN: For dinner, kids can peel the root vegetables, mix the sushi rice with vinegar and sugar, and assemble the nori rolls.

FILLINGS

1 sweet potato
3 carrots
2 parsnips
2 tablespoons olive oil
2 avocados

RICE

2 cups sushi rice
2 cups water
2 tablespoons rice vinegar
2 tablespoons pure cane sugar
1 teaspoon kosher salt

TO ASSEMBLE

5 to 6 nori sheets
Low-sodium soy sauce
Pickled ginger
Wasabi

1. You want to get the vegetables in the oven first, as they take the longest to cook. To save time, you can always peel and slice the root vegetables the night before and store them in a bowl full of cold water in the refrigerator. Preheat the oven to 425°F. Peel the root vegetables and slice them into 3-inch sticks. Toss the vegetable sticks with olive oil and a sprinkling of salt, then arrange them in a single layer on a baking sheet. Roast for 20 minutes, until tender and edges begin to brown.
2. While the veggies roast, prepare the rice. Combine the sushi rice and water in a medium saucepan over high heat. Bring to a boil, uncovered, then reduce the heat to low and cover the pan. Cook the rice for 15 minutes, then remove the pot from the heat and let it stand, covered, for 10 minutes.
3. Whisk together the vinegar, sugar, and salt in a small bowl. Pour the vinegar mixture over the rice and toss with a fork to thoroughly combine.
4. When you are ready to assemble the sushi rolls, pit and slice the avocados. Set up a rolling station with the roasted root vegetables, sliced avocado, sushi rice, nori wrappers, and a small bowl of water close at hand. To roll, cover a nori sheet with a layer of sushi rice, leaving one-quarter of

(continued)

the sheet clear. Next, pile up a horizontal strip of roasted root vegetables and avocado slices in the middle of the sushi rice. To roll, wet the top of the exposed nori sheet, then fold the bottom of the sheet in on itself, tightly rolling it along to the top. Seal and lay the roll on a cutting board. Slice with a wet, sharp knife. Serve the sushi with low-sodium soy sauce, pickled ginger, and wasabi.

FOR BABY: Infants can enjoy a bowl of rice topped with smashed or minced vegetables and sprinkled with bits of nori.

TOMORROW'S DINNER: WINTER TACOS

Double the amount of vegetables you roast for the sushi rolls so that you have leftovers. Tomorrow night, make tacos with black beans, tortillas, roasted root vegetables, and toppings (avocado, sour cream, cheese, lime, and cilantro).

QUICK MISO SOUP

serves 4 to 6

This Quick Miso Soup is a favorite of mine, as it takes only about 15 minutes from pot to bowl and has the deep, earthy flavors I love.

6 cups water
½ ounce dried bonito flakes
6 tablespoons miso paste (white or red)
8 ounces firm tofu, cut into ½-inch cubes
¼ cup finely chopped dried wakame seaweed (if it is too brittle to chop with a knife, use kitchen shears instead)
4 scallions, white and light green parts only, thinly sliced, for serving
1 tablespoon sesame seeds, for serving

1. Combine the water and bonito flakes in a medium saucepan and bring the mixture to a boil. Turn the heat down to a gentle simmer and cook the broth for 5 minutes. Turn off the heat and let the pot sit for 5 more minutes.
2. Strain the broth through a fine-mesh sieve, discard the bonito flakes, and return the clear broth to the pot over low heat. In a small bowl, whisk together the miso paste and ⅓ cup of the warm broth. Pour the miso mix into the soup, then drop in the tofu cubes, seaweed, and scallions. Cook until the seaweed becomes soft in the soup, about 5 minutes. Serve the miso soup warm, sprinkled with sesame seeds.

BANANA MILK WITH FLAX SEEDS

makes 2 glasses

This recipe is our boys' favorite nightcap (as I write this I can hear a little one-year-old voice requesting "nana milk"). This thick smoothie is blended up in a minute and is full of fragrant winter spice, healthy fats, and fiber. Tailor the banana milk to your infant's stage, choosing from yogurt, almond milk, hemp milk, coconut milk, cow's milk, or even goat's milk.

- 2 ripe bananas
- 2 cups whole cow's milk (or whatever type of milk you like)
- ½ teaspoon pure vanilla extract
- ½ teaspoon ground cinnamon
- 1 tablespoon flax seeds

OPTIONAL ADD-INS

- 1 tablespoon unsweetened shredded coconut
- 1 tablespoon nut or seed butter
- 2 dates
- Small handful of nuts
- 1 tablespoon unsweetened cocoa powder

---

1. Using a powerful blender, simply blend all the ingredients together until smooth. Pour into two glasses and enjoy. Banana Milk with Flax Seeds is best sipped down right away, as the drink slowly separates.

A Light and Colorful Winter Meal

GADO GADO SALAD

BROILED HONEY-VANILLA GRAPEFRUITS

There comes a point every winter when I start craving fresh, raw foods rather than rich roasts. Maybe my body is looking forward to spring or is telling me to load up on naturally detoxifying raw fruits and vegetables to help ward off an impending cold. Either way, it is always a nice change to enjoy a dinner like this Gado Gado Salad, full of crisp and crunchy carrots and cabbage, followed by a dessert like these Broiled Honey-Vanilla Grapefruits, bursting with tart, coral-pink juices. I pull together this brightly colored meal when I'm having one of those *winter is all gray, wet, and sad* kinds of days, and it always seems to do the trick.

GADO GADO SALAD

serves 4

This "salad" is made of simple-to-prepare and kid-friendly elements like rice and hard-boiled eggs. However, if your child just eats a pile of sliced mango and peanut-sauced rice, don't beat yourself up about it—every element of this meal is a whole and nutritious food.

KIDS CAN: Put kids in charge of measuring out the peanut sauce ingredients into the blender. They can also prepare the salad toppings with child-safe knives or kitchen shears.

SALAD

1½ cups brown rice, medium or short grain

8 cups water

1 tablespoon unsalted butter

1 teaspoon kosher salt

4 to 8 large eggs (however many your family wants)

4 carrots, peeled and cut into thin matchsticks or peeled into ribbons

2 mangoes, peeled, pitted, and thinly sliced

½ head purple cabbage, thinly sliced

1 cup cilantro leaves

1 cup dry roasted, lightly salted peanuts, chopped

SAUCE

¼ cup sesame seeds

¼ cup creamy peanut butter

5 tablespoons soy sauce

2 tablespoons rice vinegar

1 tablespoon honey

1 tablespoon minced fresh gingerroot

2 garlic cloves

5 tablespoons warm water

---

1. I like to boil my rice like pasta, as it always comes out perfectly and never sticks to the pan. Simply combine the rice and water in a saucepan. Bring the pot to a boil and let the rice cook away until tender, about 30 minutes. Drain, return the rice to the pot, stir in butter and salt, and cover until you are ready to assemble the salad. Fluff the rice with a fork before dishing it out.

2. While the rice cooks, cook the eggs. Put the eggs in the bottom of a medium pot and cover with water by 1 inch. Cover the pot and bring the water to a boil. As soon as the water starts to boil, turn off the heat and set a timer for 12 minutes. After 12 minutes, drain the eggs, run them under cold water, and peel. (If you like a soft yolk, set the timer for 8 minutes instead of 12.) Slice the peeled eggs and set them aside.

3. To make the sauce, simply whiz everything together in a blender.

4. You can assemble individual Gado Gado Salad bowls or make one large, family-style bowl. Either way, make a pile of rice, top it with carrots, mango, cabbage, cilantro, peanuts, and sliced eggs, then drizzle on some peanut

sauce. Extra peanut sauce can be kept in a sealed glass jar in the refrigerator for a few weeks. The sauce will become thick when chilled, so loosen it up with a splash of hot water or let it sit out on your counter to come to room temperature before using.

FOR BABY: Prepare a baby-friendly salad of brown rice, crumbled egg, and finely diced mango.

TOMORROW'S DINNER: NOODLE SALAD

Prepare extra toppings and store them in the refrigerator. Tomorrow night, cook some soba noodles and mix in the mango, shredded cabbage, carrots, and cilantro. Throw in diced chicken or drained chickpeas. Toss everything together and drizzle with soy sauce, sesame oil, lime juice, and sesame seeds.

BROILED HONEY-VANILLA GRAPEFRUITS

serves 4

It's always hard to find a fresh, bright dessert in the middle of winter. This is my best go of it—tart pink grapefruit halves covered with vanilla honey and roasted until gooey. The result is a treat that is both warming and refreshing.

KIDS CAN: Kids can mix and spread vanilla honey onto the grapefruit halves.

---

2 grapefruits, halved

4 tablespoons honey

½ teaspoon pure vanilla extract

---

1. Set a rack about 3 inches from the broiler and set the oven to Broil. While the broiler heats, use a serrated knife to separate the grapefruit sections from the membranes. In a small bowl, mix together the honey and vanilla, then spread the mixture evenly across the cut side of each grapefruit half (the back of a small metal spoon works best). Place the fruits in a baking dish, cut sides up, and transfer them to the rack closest to the broiler. Broil until golden and bubbly, about 4 minutes.

Our Favorite Veggie Burgers

BLACK BEAN QUINOA BURGERS

ROASTED CARROTS WITH HONEY BUTTER

QUICK CITRUS-DARK CHOCOLATE CAKE

For this menu, I've paired my family's most requested veggie burgers with roasted carrots tossed in honey butter and quick chocolate cake. This is just the kind of meal I would aim for if my husband's January birthday fell on a hectic weeknight—special but totally doable with proper planning. If you don't have any winter birthdays in your family, this dessert is perfect for the holidays or as a post-snow shoveling reward to yourself.

BLACK BEAN QUINOA BURGERS

makes 4 burgers

These burgers have been the most popular meal in our house for ten years, ever since my sister served Nick and me her version when we were first dating. Now I find myself mixing up a batch every time I feel like we have nothing for dinner, quickly realizing that quinoa, black beans, and an onion are almost always in the pantry.

KIDS CAN: Little helpers can squish the burger mixture together with their hands.

½ cup dry quinoa
1 cup water
3 tablespoons olive oil, divided
½ medium yellow onion, finely chopped
2 garlic cloves, finely chopped
One 14-ounce can black beans, drained and rinsed
½ cup panko bread crumbs
1 large egg
1 teaspoon kosher salt
1 teaspoon ground cumin
1 teaspoon chili powder
1 tablespoon tomato paste
Suggested burger toppings: sliced avocado, sprouts, honey mustard, hot sauce

---

1. Combine the quinoa and water in a small saucepan. Cover the pot and bring to a boil over high heat, then reduce the heat to low and simmer until the water is absorbed, about 15 minutes.
2. Meanwhile, heat 1 tablespoon of the olive oil in a medium sauté pan. Sauté the onion and garlic until soft, about 5 minutes.
3. In a medium bowl, combine the black beans, bread crumbs, egg, salt, cumin, chili powder, and tomato paste. Add in the cooked quinoa and the sautéed onion and garlic. Using your hands, squish the mixture together until everything is well incorporated. Form 4 equal-size patties. Heat the remaining 2 tablespoons of oil in a large skillet over medium heat. Cook the burgers in the hot oil until they are brown and crisp, about 7 minutes a side. Serve with sliced avocado, sprouts, and honey mustard or hot sauce.

FOR BABY: Crumble up a quinoa burger into bits for spoon or finger feeding. Before tossing carrots in the honey butter, smash a few plain roasted carrots with the back of a fork.

TOMORROW'S DINNER: HASH AND EGGS

Prepare a second batch of quinoa burger mix and store it in the refrigerator. Tomorrow, heat a large skillet with a couple tablespoons of olive oil and spread the mix out in a single layer, cooking it into a crispy hash. Serve the quinoa-bean hash with eggs and a salad.

ROASTED CARROTS WITH HONEY BUTTER

serves 4 to 6

Some say that eating root vegetables (like carrots) makes us feel physically and mentally grounded and rooted. In the winter, I'll take all the help I can get. Here, carrot spears are roasted then tossed in a soft honey butter, making a warm, melty, sweet, and salty side dish.

KIDS CAN: Little helpers can make the honey butter.

---

10 to 12 carrots, peeled

2 to 3 tablespoons olive oil

Kosher salt and freshly ground black pepper

2 tablespoons unsalted butter, at room temperature

2 tablespoons honey

---

1. Preheat the oven to 450°F. While the oven warms, cut the peeled carrots on the diagonal into 2-inch-long slices. Toss the carrots with olive oil, a big pinch of salt, and a few grinds of pepper. Arrange the carrots in a single layer in a roasting pan, transfer them to the oven, and roast for 20 to 30 minutes, until the edges are deeply caramelized.
2. While the carrots roast, mash the butter and honey together in a large serving bowl. Toss the roasted carrots in the honey butter, taste for salt, and serve hot.

QUICK CITRUS–DARK CHOCOLATE CAKE

makes one 8-inch round cake

This cake is as dense and rich as a fudge brownie, but it's made with antioxidant-rich dark chocolate and unrefined coconut sugar for a healthier take on a flourless chocolate dessert. A thin slice goes a long way. I like to top the cake with fresh whipped cream and thin blood orange slices for a citrus kick.

---

7 ounces dark chocolate (60 to 70% cacao)

14 tablespoons unsalted butter, cut into 1-inch cubes

1⅓ cups coconut sugar

5 large eggs

1 tablespoon unbleached all-purpose flour

3 tablespoons freshly squeezed orange juice

Whipped cream and thinly sliced blood orange, for serving

---

1. Preheat the oven to 375°F and butter an 8-inch round cake pan. Line the base of the cake pan with parchment paper.
2. Finely chop the chocolate with a serrated knife. Place the chopped chocolate in a small saucepan with the butter and gently melt the mixture over low heat, stirring regularly. Add the coconut sugar to the melted chocolate-butter mixture, stir well, and set the saucepan aside to cool for a few moments.
3. Add the eggs one by one to the chocolate mixture, whisking well after each addition. Add the flour and orange juice and stir to combine. Pour the batter into the prepared cake pan and bake for approximately 20 to 25 minutes, or until the center of the cake looks just set and the top looks shiny and a bit crackly.
4. Remove the cake from the oven and let it cool in the pan on a wire rack for 10 minutes, then carefully invert the cake onto the wire rack and peel off the parchment paper. Allow the cake to cool completely (or the whipped cream will melt right off). The cake will deflate slightly as it cools. Serve the rich cake topped with whipped cream and blood orange slices.

The Moriartys' Family Meal, St. Johnsbury, Vermont

CHICKEN TORTILLA SOUP

CHURROS WITH MEXICAN CHOCOLATE DIPPING SAUCE

---

shared by Ashleigh Moriarty

When I was growing up, my English mom made a complete roast dinner every Sunday, which always made our house feel comforting and cozy. Now that I have my own family, I try to carry on this tradition as often as possible. Our very long, cold Vermont winters make it a necessity to cook meals that fill the family and house with warmth. This Chicken Tortilla Soup is a perfect snowy day recipe, but don't be afraid to make it in other seasons, as the flavors complement the warm spring and summer months as well. In fact, the first time we had Chicken Tortilla Soup was on a sweltering beach in Mexico. Perhaps we make this often in the cold winter to try to channel that beachy feeling again.

CHICKEN TORTILLA SOUP

serves 4 to 6

Whenever I roast a whole chicken, I use the leftovers to make a rich broth for the base of this soup. I put the picked-over chicken carcass in the slow cooker and let it cook for 8 to 12 hours to make an easy, hands-off stock. Our daughters help prepare all the yummy soup garnishes, such as the tortillas, grated cheese, and cilantro. They especially enjoy this interactive dinner, as they are able to pick and pile on whatever toppings they like.

KIDS CAN: Kids can prepare the tortilla strips by slicing the corn tortillas with a pizza cutter, tossing them in oil, and arranging them on a baking sheet.

---

1 medium yellow onion

2 garlic cloves

½ to 1 jalapeño pepper, seeds and membranes removed

3 tablespoons olive oil, divided

One 14-ounce can diced tomatoes

1 teaspoon plus a pinch of kosher salt, divided

6 cups Slow Cooker Chicken Stock (recipe follows) or low-sodium chicken broth

4 cups shredded chicken (from a 4- to 5-pound roasted chicken)

Juice of 1 lime

8 small corn tortillas

SLOW COOKER CHICKEN STOCK

One 4- to 5-pound chicken, roasted, meat removed

2 celery ribs

2 carrots

2 medium onions, halved

2 bay leaves

Small handful herbs of your choice (such as parsley or thyme), optional

TOPPINGS

Sour cream

Lime wedges

Chopped cilantro

Sliced avocado

Hot sauce

---

1. To make the stock, place the chicken carcass, celery, carrots, onions, and bay leaves in a 6-quart slow cooker. Add any herbs. Cover with water and cook on low for at least 8 and up to 24 hours. Using a fine-mesh sieve, strain the finished stock into a large pot.
2. When you're ready to make the soup, preheat the oven to 375°F. In a food processor, whiz the onion, garlic, and jalapeño into a fine paste.
3. Heat 2 tablespoons of the oil in a large soup pot over medium heat and sauté the onion mixture until soft, 5 to 7 minutes. Add the tomatoes, 1 teaspoon of the salt, the broth, shredded chicken, and lime juice. Bring the soup to a boil, reduce the heat to low, and simmer for 5 minutes or until everything is heated through.
4. Slice the corn tortillas into ¼-inch-thick strips

(continued)

(this is easy with a pizza cutter). In a large bowl, toss the tortilla strips with the remaining 1 tablespoon of oil and the remaining pinch of salt, then arrange them in a single layer on a rimmed baking sheet. Toast the tortilla strips in the oven until crisp, about 10 minutes. To serve, place some tortilla strips in the bottom of each bowl, ladle the soup over the top, and pile on the toppings.

FOR BABY: Depending on your baby's age and tastes, omit or reduce the amount of jalapeño in the soup. Pulse a bowl of soup and a few avocado slices in the food processor, or whiz the mixture with an immersion blender to create a creamy consistency. Older infants can enjoy the soup as is.

CHURROS WITH MEXICAN CHOCOLATE DIPPING SAUCE

makes 18 churros

This dessert is popular in our house because the girls can, to their delight, make the churros themselves with minimal supervision.

KIDS CAN: Little helpers can prepare the churros by sprinkling on the cinnamon-sugar mixture, then cutting and twisting the dough.

CHURROS

½ cup pure cane sugar

2 tablespoons ground cinnamon

1 sheet frozen puff pastry dough, defrosted

MEXICAN CHOCOLATE DIPPING SAUCE

½ cup heavy cream

¾ cup chopped Mexican chocolate (Taza Cacao Puro is our favorite)

Pinch of ground cinnamon

Up to ½ teaspoon cayenne or ancho chili powder (optional, depending on your family's heat tolerance)

---

1. To make the churros, preheat the oven to 375°F. Mix the sugar and cinnamon together in a small bowl. Sprinkle half of the mixture over a sheet of parchment paper and lay the defrosted puff pastry on top. Cut the puff pastry into 1-inch-thick strips (the short way) and brush them with water. Sprinkle the wet strips with the remaining cinnamon-sugar mixture. Hold both ends of each strip and twist it 2 to 3 times before placing it on a baking sheet. Repeat with the remaining strips. Bake for 20 minutes or until puffy and golden.

2. While the churros are baking, combine the cream and chocolate in a small saucepan and warm the mixture over low heat, whisking constantly until the chocolate begins to melt, about 3 minutes. Stir in the cinnamon and chili powder (if using). Continue whisking until the chocolate is melted and the ingredients are combined, about 5 minutes. Serve the churros with individual pots of warm dipping sauce.

Kids Eating Fish

COD CAKES WITH POACHED EGGS

QUICK ARUGULA SALAD

SLOW COOKER BROWN RICE PUDDING

Once Columbus Day comes and goes, many shops, restaurants, and homes around us lock up for the next seven months. Thankfully, a handful of our favorite spots stay open to support us through this most trying stretch. There is a diner in town that we frequent on cold, early mornings—we run into friends, drink too much coffee, and say yes to the boys' requests of chocolate chip pancakes. My menu favorite is a codfish cake served with poached eggs and greens. This winter meal is inspired by that favorite diner breakfast. The cakes' crispy, golden edges and potato filling help to convince all family members that a crispy fish cake is worth trying.

COD CAKES WITH POACHED EGGS

serves 4

Our kids love New England clam chowder, but it's a challenge to hook them on other seafood dinners (you ironic island kids, you). These cakes are my best attempt at getting some fish into our boys—sometimes it succeeds, and other times one of them ends up eating a couple of eggs for dinner. Such is life. I like my cod cake with a runny poached egg, but sunny-side up or scrambled eggs are just as good. A quick arugula salad pairs well with this rich dish. I just toss baby arugula with olive oil, lemon juice, salt, and pepper.

---

1 tablespoon fresh thyme leaves
3 tablespoons minced fresh chives
2 tablespoons Dijon mustard
1 tablespoon real mayonnaise
1 teaspoon kosher salt
½ teaspoon freshly grated orange zest
1 to 2 large Yukon gold potatoes, peeled and cut into 1-inch cubes (about 2 cups)
1 pound filleted codfish
¾ cup panko bread crumbs
¼ cup extra virgin olive oil
Splash of white vinegar
4 large eggs
Lemon wedges, for serving

---

1. In a medium bowl, combine the thyme, chives, mustard, mayonnaise, salt, and orange zest. Stir everything to combine.
2. Place the cubed potatoes in a large, high-sided skillet and cover with water. Bring the water to a boil over high heat, reduce the heat to low, cover, and simmer the potatoes until tender, about 7 minutes. Using a slotted spoon, remove the cooked potatoes from the skillet and place them in a small bowl. Do not drain the skillet. Mash the potatoes with a fork and set them aside.
3. Return the skillet to the stove over high heat, bring the potato cooking water to a boil, and then carefully slide in the cod fillets. Turn the heat down to the lowest setting, cover, and poach the fish until just flaky and cooked through, about 5 minutes. Remove from the water and gently flake the fish apart, then fold it into the mashed potatoes. Add the potato-cod mixture to the mustard mixture and add in the bread crumbs. Carefully fold everything to combine (you want to keep big flakes of fish).
4. Heat the olive oil in a large cast iron skillet set over medium heat. While it heats, use your hands to divide the cod cake mixture into four large patties. Cook the cakes in the hot oil for 5 to 7 minutes per side or until crisp and golden.
5. While the cakes fry up, poach your eggs. Fill a pot with a few inches of water and add the vinegar. Put the pot over medium-high heat and

warm it until the water is just starting to bubble or simmer. This is the temperature you want to stick with. Crack the first egg into a small bowl or ramekin. Gently slide the egg into the hot water and let it cook for 3 to 4 minutes. Remove the egg with a slotted spoon and place it directly onto a kitchen towel to absorb any excess water. Repeat this process with the rest of the eggs. You can cook more than one egg at a time if your pot is large enough.

6. Place a poached egg on the top of each cod cake and serve immediately with lemon wedges and a quick arugula salad (see the note in the recipe's introduction).

FOR BABY: The soft texture of cod cakes is perfect for baby. Either mix a runny poached egg into baby's cod cake or prepare an egg in their favorite style to serve on the side.

TOMORROW'S DINNER: GREEN HOME FRIES

Boil a second pot of potatoes. Tomorrow, place a large cast iron skillet over medium-high heat. Add some butter, sliced cooked potatoes, and 4 cups of baby spinach. Cook until the potatoes are crisp and the spinach is wilted, 7 to 10 minutes. Eat with local sausages, bacon, and/or eggs.

SLOW COOKER BROWN RICE PUDDING

serves 4 to 6

This rice pudding is one of my favorite winter treats, as you simply mix the ingredients together in the slow cooker, turn it on, and later that day enjoy a warm, nutritious pudding without lifting a finger. Bonus—your house smells like a bakery.

KIDS CAN: In the morning, little ones can measure the rice pudding ingredients into the slow cooker, and after dinner kids can whip the cream, crush the pecans, and shave the dark chocolate with a vegetable peeler.

¾ cup long-grain brown rice

4½ cups whole milk, divided

¾ cup coconut sugar (or any granulated sweetener)

1 teaspoon ground cinnamon

1 teaspoon pure vanilla extract

Pinch of kosher salt

5 tablespoons unsalted butter, melted

FOR SERVING (OPTIONAL)

Whipped cream

Chopped pecans

Shaved dark chocolate

---

1. In a 6-quart slow cooker, mix together the rice, 3½ cups of the milk, the sugar, cinnamon, vanilla, salt, and melted butter. Cover the slow cooker and cook on high for 4 to 4½ hours, until the rice is tender (taste the rice around 4 hours). Just before serving, stir in the remaining cup of milk. Top the pudding with whipped cream, chopped pecans, and dark chocolate shavings.

FOR BABY: Brown rice pudding is a soft, sweet treat babies can enjoy.

Orange and Green Pasta Bowls

CREAMY PUMPKIN FETTUCCINE

PUMPKIN SEED PESTO

ROASTED BROCCOLINI

Winter food cravings are serious things, not to be ignored. You can't help but dream of cheesy casseroles, warming soups, and rich chocolate after shoveling feet of snow, turning on the lights at 4 P.M., and slathering moisturizer on dry, patchy skin, day after day. We need incentives to keep up with life's pace in unapologetic weather (and I'm not just talking wine here). This dinner has all those things we look for in winter comfort food, but also offers healthy doses of spinach, nutrient-dense pumpkin seeds, and Broccolini. I like to eat the Creamy Pumpkin Fettuccine, Pumpkin Seed Pesto, and Roasted Broccolini piled high together in one bowl. Extra pesto is delicious in omelets, as a sandwich spread, or tossed with roasted root vegetables.

CREAMY PUMPKIN FETTUCCINE

serves 4 to 6

This pasta dinner offers two delicious sauces—creamy pumpkin and Pumpkin Seed Pesto (recipe follows). Ideally, you would eat the fettuccine tossed in the creamy pumpkin sauce with a dollop of pesto on top. That said, if you have time for only one sauce, or if your family naturally gravitates to one type over the other, the fettuccine is delicious served with either one. To make the most of your time, prepare the pesto and get the Broccolini in the oven right when you put the pot of pasta water on to boil.

KIDS CAN: Little helpers can whisk together the cream sauce ingredients.

½ pound dried fettuccine

½ pound dried spinach fettuccine

5 ounces grated Parmesan cheese, plus more for serving

3 tablespoons heavy cream

1 large egg

⅔ cup pureed cooked or canned pumpkin (or any winter squash)

1 teaspoon arrowroot powder or cornstarch

3 tablespoons extra virgin olive oil, plus more for serving

½ teaspoon freshly grated lemon zest

Kosher salt and freshly ground black pepper

Pumpkin Seed Pesto (recipe follows)

---

1. Bring a big pot of salted water to a boil over high heat. When the water comes to a rolling boil, cook the pastas together per the package instructions, shaving 1 minute off the suggested cooking time. Just before draining the pasta, scoop 1 cup of hot pasta water from the pot and reserve it for the sauce. Drain the pasta and set it aside.
2. While the pasta cooks, whisk together the Parmesan cheese, cream, egg, pureed pumpkin, arrowroot powder, olive oil, and lemon zest in a medium bowl. Whisk in the reserved pasta water. Season the sauce with salt and pepper.
3. Return your pasta pot to medium-high heat and pour in the sauce. Bring the pumpkin sauce to a boil, then turn down the heat to a simmer. Cook the sauce for 2 to 3 minutes, just until it has thickened, then add the pasta to the pot. Toss the pasta and sauce together and serve it with dollops of Pumpkin Seed Pesto and the Roasted Broccolini (recipes follow).

PUMPKIN SEED PESTO

makes about 1½ cups

The best thing about pesto is that it is, almost always, green. Because of this, when a new bowl of vibrant pesto sauce hits our dinner table, the boys don't question the ingredients as long as they see that familiar green color. We have experimented with a wide variety of pestos at our house, from kale to artichoke and sun-dried tomato. This rich and nutty Pumpkin Seed Pesto is my favorite thing for adding a salty bite to creamy pastas and soups.

1 cup toasted pumpkin seeds
1½ cups baby spinach
Zest and juice of 1 lemon
1 garlic clove
½ teaspoon kosher salt
¼ cup extra virgin olive oil

1. Simply whiz everything together in a food processor. Extra pesto can be stored in an airtight glass jar in the refrigerator for up to 1 week.

TOMORROW'S DINNER: PANINI

Slice a loaf of hearty, whole-wheat bread. Spread the slices with leftover pesto, then layer on Monterey Jack cheese, sliced turkey breast, and sliced tomatoes. Grill in a lightly buttered cast iron skillet, weighting the sandwiches down with a heavy pot.

ROASTED BROCCOLINI

serves 4

Broccolini is similar to broccoli but with smaller florets and long, thin stalks. Many cultures stir-fry the vegetable (which is delicious), but I like to roast it in the oven, as the stalks hold up well under high heat. Nutritionally, it is high in vitamin C and contains vitamin A, calcium, folate, and iron.

KIDS CAN: Children can toss the Broccolini with the oil and salt.

- 1 bunch Broccolini, trimmed
- 1 tablespoon olive oil
- Big pinch kosher salt

1. Preheat the oven to 400°F. Toss the Broccolini with the olive oil and salt. Arrange the Broccolini in an even layer on a baking sheet. Roast until crisp and tender, about 20 minutes.

FOR BABY: Make a small bowl of pumpkin pasta, Broccolini, and pesto for baby. Finely chop or whiz the dinner in a food processor to create the ideal texture. For older infants, chopped Broccolini is an easy finger food.

Winter Sunday Supper (and a Campfire Party)

KALE AND SWEET POTATO TACOS

CORN TORTILLAS

SLOW COOKER BLACK BEANS

HONEY MARSHMALLOWS

Before we moved to Martha's Vineyard, we lived in Providence, Rhode Island. I worked downtown, right around the corner from a great little taco shop. Nick's grad-school building was a short walk away, so every Friday we would meet and treat ourselves to a taco lunch. I always ordered the special veggie taco of the day—piled high with kale ribbons, roasted sweet potatoes, or charred mushrooms. This dinner reminds me of that time of our lives, however far off it feels today.

KALE AND SWEET POTATO TACOS

serves 6

For these tacos, we layer warm vegetables, slightly sweet black beans (made in the slow cooker!), and avocado cream onto homemade corn tortillas. If you have a lazy Sunday, it's fun to make all the components yourself, but without the time it's fine to use store-bought tortillas and canned beans instead.

TACO FILLINGS

3 sweet potatoes

1 large bunch kale

3 tablespoons olive oil, divided

Kosher salt

⅓ cup water

AVOCADO CREAM

2 avocados

2 tablespoons sour cream or plain full-fat yogurt

Juice from ½ lime

2 big pinches kosher salt

Slow Cooker Black Beans (page 82)

Corn Tortillas (page 80)

1 cup chopped fresh cilantro, for serving

Hot sauce, for serving

Lime wedges, for serving

1. Prepare the vegetables. Peel the potatoes and dice them into ⅛-inch cubes (they need to be small to cook through in the skillet). Prepare the kale by removing the stems and slicing the leaves into thin ribbons. Heat 2 tablespoons of the oil in a large cast iron skillet over medium heat. Add the potatoes, sprinkle with salt, and spread them out in a single layer. Cover the skillet (use a baking sheet if you don't have a large lid), and cook for 10 minutes (tossing once), until fork-tender. Add in the kale ribbons, another sprinkle of salt, and the water. Toss to combine, cover again, and cook for another 10 minutes, until the kale is wilted (tossing once). Taste and add more salt if needed.
2. While the vegetables are cooking, make the avocado cream. Do this by mashing the avocados, sour cream, lime juice, and salt together in a small bowl.
3. To serve, pile black beans and vegetables into fresh corn tortillas. Top with avocado cream, chopped cilantro, hot sauce, and a squirt of fresh lime juice.

FOR BABY: In a small bowl, mash together some sweet potato, kale, and beans. Spoon-feed the mixture while baby holds and munches on a soft tortilla.

TOMORROW'S DINNER: VEGETABLE FRITTATA

Prepare a second skillet of sweet potatoes and kale. Tomorrow, mix the vegetables with 7 whisked eggs, ⅓ cup of milk, ⅓ cup of cream, salt, pepper, and a dash of Worcestershire sauce. Transfer the mixture to an oven-safe skillet and bake at 375°F until set, about 25 minutes.

CORN TORTILLAS

makes about 12 tortillas

If you don't already own a tortilla press, it is one of the one-trick kitchen gadgets I recommend. They are inexpensive, easy to use, and make the most delicious homemade corn tortillas. Kids will especially love rolling out and pressing the soft tortilla dough.

---

2 cups masa harina (we like Bob's Red Mill Masa Harina Golden Corn Flour)

½ teaspoon kosher salt

1½ to 2 cups water

---

1. In a large mixing bowl, stir together the masa harina and salt. Add 1¼ to 1½ cups of the water, a little at a time, stirring between each addition until the dough just comes together into a ball. Cover the bowl with plastic wrap and let it sit at room temperature for 15 to 30 minutes. At this point the dough will be too dry and crumbly to work with. Add the remaining ½ to ¾ cup of water, a little at a time, and mix until you can make smooth balls of the dough without its sticking to your hands. Cover the bowl and set it aside.
2. Preheat two large skillets, one over medium-high heat and one over high heat.
3. Line a shallow bowl with a large, clean kitchen towel. Cut a plastic bag into two rounds about the size of the tortilla press. Place a 1-inch ball of dough in the center of the first piece of plastic. Press down on the dough to flatten it some. If the dough cracks at this point, it's a little too dry: return the dough to the ball, mix in a little more water, and start again. Add the second piece of plastic on top of the flattened dough, then transfer the dough and plastic to the tortilla press and press the tortilla firmly. Open it, rotate the tortilla 90 degrees, and press it again. Peel off the top piece of plastic. Carefully peel the tortilla off the bottom piece of plastic and place it in the skillet set over medium-high heat. Once it sets and can be slid around (after about 1 minute), flip the tortilla and transfer it to the skillet set over high heat. When the tortilla puffs slightly, flip it again (keeping it over high heat) and cook for another 30 seconds until it gets a nice color and puffs a little more. Transfer the tortilla to the kitchen towel–lined bowl and fold the towel over it. Repeat this process with the remaining tortilla dough, keeping the warm tortillas under wraps of the towel. It goes pretty fast once you get into a rhythm. Extra corn tortillas can be wrapped tightly and stored on the counter for up to 2 days. To reheat, dampen the tortillas with wet hands and warm them in a skillet.

SLOW COOKER BLACK BEANS

makes 6 cups

I was always intimidated by cooking dried beans. I would either forget to soak them ahead of time (AHHHH!) or keep them simmering in a pot, only to find them undercooked at the end of the day. After a while, I began to shy away from recipes that suggested I try it again. Discovering the simplicity of preparing dried beans in the slow cooker has thrown my trepidation out the window. You just combine a few ingredients and turn on the machine—a few hours later you have a perfect pot of beans. Life changing.

2 cups dried black beans, picked over and rinsed
4 cups water
1 teaspoon ground cumin
½ teaspoon kosher salt (plus more to finish)
3 garlic cloves
½ medium yellow onion
¼ navel orange

1. Combine everything in a 6-quart slow cooker, cover, and cook on high for 4 hours. After 4 hours, turn the slow cooker to the "keep warm" setting until you're ready to eat. Taste and add more salt if needed.

HONEY MARSHMALLOWS

makes 60 to 100 marshmallows, depending on size

The winter months are isolating, so I try to find any excuse to lure friends over to our house. These Honey Marshmallows are a treat we make on lazy weekends to roast outside over a simple campfire with friends. The process of making homemade marshmallows is as much a fun science experiment as a dessert. It naturally pulls the kids into the kitchen. Marshmallows are typically full of refined sugar, but these beauties are mostly water and honey.

KIDS CAN: Kids will love helping with all the marshmallow steps, including watching the mix turn into marshmallow cream and dusting the squares with powdered sugar.

1 tablespoon canola oil, plus more for cutting the marshmallow

3 tablespoons gelatin

1 cup water, divided

1 cup honey

1½ teaspoons pure vanilla extract (see Note)

1 cup confectioners' sugar, for dusting

NOTE: You can replace vanilla with another extract, such as peppermint, orange, or almond, using more or less depending on the potency of the extract.

1. Grease a 13 by 9-inch baking dish with 1 tablespoon of oil and line it with parchment paper.

2. In the bowl of a stand mixer, whisk together the gelatin and ½ cup of the water. Let sit until the gelatin softens up, about 5 minutes.

3. In a small saucepan, combine the remaining ½ cup of water with the honey and vanilla. Clip a candy thermometer to the inside of the pan and bring the mixture to a boil over medium-high heat until it reaches 240°F (the soft ball stage), about 10 minutes. As soon as it reaches 240°F, turn the mixer on low and pour the hot honey mixture into the gelatin while beating. Increase the mixer speed to high and beat until fluffy marshmallow cream forms, about 10 minutes. Pour the whipped marshmallow into the prepared baking dish and smooth the top. Leave the pan on the counter to set for at least 4 or up to 24 hours.

4. When you are ready to cut the marshmallow, dust your countertop with the confectioners' sugar. Invert the marshmallow out of the pan onto the sugar. Peel away the parchment paper. Grease a knife with canola oil and slice the marshmallow into 1 to 2-inch squares. Toss the cut marshmallows in a pile of confectioners' sugar. Extra marshmallows can be stored at room temperature in an airtight, parchment paper–lined tin for up to two weeks.

Spring

Spring is the universal light at the end of the tunnel. It is the prize for once again surviving a cold, dark winter, and in our case, one on an island with two very energetic young boys. I spend most of February daydreaming about stepping off the front porch into a sixty-degree day, and when it finally happens—man oh man—nothing is better. I have an idealistic view of spring on which I place many of my hopes: "Oh, he'll sleep until 7 A.M. in the spring" and "I will never feel overwhelmed in May!" are some of my optimistic thoughts. The funny thing is, most of the time the season lives up to my expectations (well, not the 7 A.M. part), and even when it doesn't, the strawberries, asparagus, and hours in the dirt overwhelm me with gratitude and make me forget my worries. Spring dinners are lighter (Oven-Baked Falafel with Garden Radishes, Cucumber, and Pea Shoots, page 90) and more colorful (Leek, Red Potato, and Feta Galette, page 96), and they show off what is sprouting outside (Rhubarb Sundaes, page 100). They also offer a variety of raw, colorful foods packed with antioxidants to help detox weary winter bodies and clean out their dusty systems. When the time is right, grab a blanket and eat outside, even if it's in your driveway. We waited too long for this season to stay indoors.

Spring Meals

A Spring Picnic

OVEN-BAKED FALAFEL WITH GARDEN RADISHES, CUCUMBER, AND PEA SHOOTS

ROASTED ASPARAGUS

This is a perfect dinner for nights when your cupboards are bare (I seem to always have these ingredients hiding someplace) and your energy is low (just whiz everything in the food processor and bake). Depending on your family's likes, you can serve the falafel balls packed in pita pockets with yogurt sauce and fresh vegetables, on top of a large green salad, or on a platter next to other nibbles, such as olives, cucumbers, tomatoes, and tzatziki and hummus dips. In my opinion, there is no wrong way to eat a warm, homemade falafel ball (especially if you are doing so outside on the green grass).

OVEN-BAKED FALAFEL WITH GARDEN RADISHES, CUCUMBER, AND PEA SHOOTS

makes 15 small balls

My sister Anna made us a version of these falafel rounds almost ten years ago. I immediately quizzed her on the recipe and have been serving it ever since. Our favorite method is to fill toasted pita pockets with falafel balls, then stuff in favorite crunchy vegetables, such as carrots, sprouts, radishes, cucumbers, or pea shoots. Here, I have included a simple yogurt sauce, but spreading the pitas with hummus works fine, too.

KIDS CAN: Little helpers can measure and blend the falafel ingredients and scoop and flatten the falafel balls.

FALAFEL

½ medium yellow onion

One 15-ounce can chickpeas, drained and rinsed

Handful of fresh parsley

Juice of ½ lemon

1 teaspoon ground cumin

1 teaspoon kosher salt

¼ teaspoon red pepper flakes (optional)

3 garlic cloves

4 tablespoons whole-wheat all-purpose flour (or gluten-free all-purpose flour)

2 tablespoons olive oil, divided

YOGURT SAUCE

1 cup plain full-fat Greek yogurt

3-inch piece cucumber, grated

Juice of ½ lemon

1 tablespoon chopped fresh dill

Kosher salt and freshly ground black pepper

FOR SERVING

4 pita pockets or lavash, warmed in the oven

Thinly sliced cucumber

Thinly sliced radishes

Thinly sliced red onion

Roughly chopped pea shoots

---

1. Preheat the oven to 400°F. To make the falafel, simply whiz all the ingredients (leaving out 1 tablespoon of the olive oil) in a food processor until mostly smooth (with a few remaining chunks).

2. Grease a baking sheet with the remaining tablespoon of olive oil. Using a tablespoon measure, place heaping scoops of the falafel mixture on the baking sheet, then flatten them with the back of the spoon. Bake the falafel rounds for 10 minutes, flip them, and then bake for another 10 minutes, until edges are crisp and tops are golden.

3. While the falafel bakes, mix together all the sauce ingredients in a medium bowl.

4. Serve the baked falafel with warm pita pockets or lavash, yogurt sauce, sliced vegetables, and pea shoots.

FOR BABY: For older babies, smash a falafel ball inside a small wedge of pita bread and top with yogurt sauce. Younger babies will enjoy small pieces of falafel and thin slices of peeled cucumber.

TOMORROW'S DINNER: CHICKEN KABOBS

Grill chicken kabobs and top the skewers with extra yogurt sauce and chopped vegetables.

ROASTED ASPARAGUS

serves 4

Roasted asparagus often finds its way onto our table in the spring because stalk snapping is Dylan's favorite kitchen job. When asparagus is around, I am guaranteed a few quiet minutes to throw dinner together while he works on the floor.

KIDS CAN: Everyone can snap asparagus stalks, of course!

- 1 bunch asparagus, ends trimmed
- 2 tablespoons extra virgin olive oil
- Big pinch of kosher salt

1. Preheat the oven to 400°F. In a large bowl, toss the trimmed asparagus with the oil and salt. Arrange the spears in a single layer on a rimmed baking sheet. Roast the asparagus for 20 to 25 minutes, until tips are crisp. (You can roast them ahead, or stick them in the oven with the falafel.)

FOR BABY: Asparagus can be stringy, so chop it well before offering it as a finger food.

Frozen Pastry Crust to the Rescue

LEEK, RED POTATO, AND FETA GALETTE
SPRING SALAD WITH BUTTERMILK-HERB DRESSING
RHUBARB SUNDAES

This dinner is all about the art of frozen pastry. I highly recommend making a batch of pastry when you score fifteen extra minutes and freezing it for impromptu galettes and quiches. That way, all you have to do is toss the frozen dough in the refrigerator in the morning to defrost and, come dinnertime, fill it with any combination of vegetables, cheese, and eggs you like. For especially desperate afternoons, kids can stamp cookies from a rolled-out round of pastry dough. Simply sprinkle the stamped shapes with cinnamon and coconut sugar, then bake at 350°F until golden—that is sure to lighten the mood.

LEEK, RED POTATO, AND FETA GALETTE

serves 4 to 6

A galette is simply a flat, round, freeform pastry thing. You can fill it with whatever you'd like, and it is not supposed to look neat. Here, I combine thinly sliced red potatoes, leeks, dill, feta, and lemon for a fresh bake. I encourage you to adapt this combination to your own tastes—perhaps trying crumbled goat cheese in place of the feta or tossing in a handful of leftover crumbled bacon. Keep in mind that you will need to thaw the frozen dough in the refrigerator overnight and then allow it to warm up on the counter for 15 minutes before rolling it out.

KIDS CAN: Set up a big pot of water for kids to wash and clean the sliced leeks.

CRUST

2 cups unbleached all-purpose flour, plus more for dusting

½ teaspoon kosher salt

1 cup (2 sticks) cold unsalted butter, cut into ½-inch cubes

¼ cup ice water

FILLING

2 tablespoons extra virgin olive oil

3 leeks, white and light green parts thinly sliced (about 2½ cups)

3 medium red potatoes, sliced into ⅛-inch-thick rounds

½ teaspoon kosher salt

5 grinds of black pepper

2 tablespoons chopped fresh dill

4 tablespoons crumbled feta cheese

Juice of ½ lemon

1. To make the crust, measure the flour and salt into a food processor, then pulse a few times to combine. Add the butter cubes and continue to pulse until the butter bits are the size of peas. Next, turn the motor on and stream in the ice water, starting with ¼ cup, then adding a bit more if the dough looks really sandy. Continue to run the motor until the dough just begins to form a ball. Turn the motor off.

2. Dust a work surface with flour, then turn out the dough and gently form it into a ball. Flatten the ball into a disk. Wrap the dough in plastic and store it in the refrigerator for at least 10 minutes and up to 24 hours. (Or place the wrapped dough in the freezer to use at a future date.)

3. To make the galette, preheat the oven to 375°F.

4. Clean the sliced leeks in a large bowl of water—gritty soil often hides between the vegetable's layers. Dry the washed leeks well on a kitchen towel.

5. In a large sauté pan, warm the olive oil over medium heat. Add the dry leeks, sliced potatoes,

(continued)

salt, and pepper. Cook until the vegetables are soft, gently tossing, about 10 minutes. Turn off the heat and add in the chopped dill, crumbled feta, and lemon juice. Allow the filling to cool slightly as you roll out the pastry dough.

6. Dust the counter with flour and roll the dough disk into a 14-inch-thick round. Don't worry about creating a perfect circle! Fill the middle of the pastry with the vegetable mixture, leaving a 1-inch border of dough all the way around. Fold the border of dough up around the filling and bake for 25 to 30 minutes, until the crust is slightly golden.

FOR BABY: Older babies can happily nibble on bite-size pieces of galette. For infants needing softer foods, puree portions of the leeks and potatoes.

TOMORROW'S DINNER: VEGETABLE FRITTATA

Prepare a second batch of leeks and red potatoes in an oven-safe skillet. Mix the vegetables with 7 whisked eggs, ⅓ cup of milk, ⅓ cup of cream, salt, pepper, and a dash of Worcestershire sauce. Bake at 375°F until set, about 25 minutes.

SPRING SALAD WITH BUTTERMILK-HERB DRESSING

serves 4; makes about 1 cup

A simple salad of baby spring lettuce makes a perfect complement to the galette. Buttermilk-Herb Dressing is a special way to dress the greens. I often fill a small bowl with olives and serve them alongside the creamy salad for a little briny bite.

KIDS CAN: This dressing is a perfect project for little helpers—throw all the ingredients into a glass jar, tighten the lid, and shake, shake, shake.

DRESSING

½ cup plain full-fat Greek yogurt

½ cup buttermilk

1 tablespoon chopped fresh basil

1 tablespoon chopped fresh chives

1 tablespoon chopped fresh dill

2 teaspoons apple cider vinegar

1 teaspoon pure cane sugar

1 teaspoon Worcestershire sauce

Big pinch of kosher salt

A few grinds of black pepper

4 cups baby lettuce leaves

1. Combine all the dressing ingredients in a large jar. Screw on a tight-fitting lid and shake vigorously to combine. Gently toss the baby lettuce with 4 tablespoons dressing (add more to taste) and serve immediately. Buttermilk-Herb Dressing can be stored in the refrigerator for 1 week.

RHUBARB SUNDAES

makes about 6 sundaes

For a special end to this meal, try a quick rhubarb topping for vanilla ice cream. The fruit sauce is straightforward and creates a simple sundae reminiscent of warm pie à la mode.

KIDS CAN: At dessert time, children can mix the chutney ingredients and pick mint leaves to top the sundaes.

---

3 rhubarb stalks, finely chopped (about 2 cups)
Pinch of kosher salt
½ teaspoon pure vanilla extract
1 cinnamon stick
2 tablespoons honey
Juice of ½ lemon
Vanilla ice cream, for serving
Mint leaves, for serving (optional)
Sugar cones, for serving (optional)

---

1. Preheat the oven to 325°F. Combine the chopped rhubarb, salt, vanilla, cinnamon stick, honey, and lemon juice in a baking dish or small ovenproof saucepan. Toss the ingredients to combine and cover the dish or pan with a lid. Bake for 30 minutes, until slightly thickened and fragrant. Remove the chutney from the oven and set it aside to cool.
2. Top scoops of vanilla ice cream with warm or room-temperature rhubarb chutney, and, if desired, add a few fresh mint leaves and a little cone hat to each serving. Refrigerate extra chutney in an airtight glass jar and enjoy within 1 week.

More Peas, Please!

SWEET PEA OVEN RISOTTO

GARLICKY PEA SHOOTS

STRAWBERRIES WITH VANILLA SUGAR

There were a few years there when the boys would eat only *frozen* peas. I found this to be so odd until I wrote about it and discovered that it is a common thread among toddlers and preschoolers—who knew? Happily, that frozen pea stage upped their pea confidence, so now they are more likely to welcome the little sweet vegetable in other (warmer . . . cooked) forms. Most recently, Dylan showed me the pea shoots growing in his preschool garden and quickly requested them at dinnertime. The thin, delicate shoots are sweet, tender, and a delicious addition to any spring meal. Lucky for me, Dylan discovered this vegetable on his own, and this ownership makes him happy to see, talk about, and eat the green shoots again and again.

SWEET PEA OVEN RISOTTO

serves 6

The first time I visited Nick's childhood home in New York, my now mother-in-law, Polly, made a version of this risotto for dinner. I was so impressed by the texture of the rice that I immediately asked for the recipe. Since then, this versatile, comforting risotto has been our favorite meal to please a crowd. Here, I toss in some sweet peas, but roasted cherry tomatoes, caramelized winter squash, and sautéed mushrooms are delicious, too.

---

4 tablespoons extra virgin olive oil

4 shallots, finely chopped

2 cups Arborio rice

4½ cups low-sodium chicken broth

2 cups sweet peas (thawed if frozen, blanched in boiling water if fresh)

4 tablespoons unsalted butter

2 handfuls of freshly grated Parmesan cheese

Garlicky Pea Shoots (recipe follows), for serving

---

1. Preheat the oven to 400°F.
2. Place an oven-safe pot over medium heat. Add the olive oil and then the chopped shallots and sauté until soft but not browned. Add in the rice and cook it for a few minutes, stirring constantly, until the grains glisten.
3. Meanwhile, pour the broth into a separate saucepan, bring it to a boil, and immediately remove it from the heat. Add 4 cups of the hot broth to the rice mixture. Stir to combine and bring the rice pot to a boil, then cover the pot and transfer it to the oven. Cook for 20 minutes or until the liquid is mostly absorbed and the rice is tender. Remove the pot from the oven and add in the peas, butter, the remaining ½ cup of warm broth, and handfuls of Parmesan cheese. Stir everything to combine and serve topped with Garlicky Pea Shoots.

FOR BABY: The sweetness and soft texture of this risotto are perfect for baby. If you'd like, stir in finely chopped pea shoots for added nutrition.

TOMORROW'S DINNER: RISOTTO CAKES

Make a second pot of oven risotto (swap peas for any other favorite cooked veggie, like spinach, mushrooms, or asparagus), and let it sit in the refrigerator overnight. The rice will get firm and sticky. Form the rice into small patties and fry them in a large skillet coated with olive oil until crispy and browned on both sides.

GARLICKY PEA SHOOTS

serves 4

Thin, tender pea shoots are really delicious stir-fried over high heat until just wilted (not left over the heat too long to wither away). Here, I toss in some garlic, but a few grates of fresh ginger or a squirt of lemon juice is also tasty.

KIDS CAN: Kids can tear up the pea shoots with their hands or kitchen shears.

- 1 tablespoon extra virgin olive oil
- 1 garlic clove, minced or grated on a microplane
- 3 loosely packed cups pea shoots, torn into pieces
- Kosher salt

---

1. Heat the oil in a medium skillet over medium-high heat. Add the minced garlic and pea shoots. Continuously toss the pea shoots with garlic until they are just wilted. Sprinkle with salt and serve on top of the risotto.

STRAWBERRIES WITH VANILLA SUGAR

serves 4

Dessert in the spring really means one thing—strawberries. The wild turkeys always eat the ripe berries from our plants, but happily, farm stands are not far away. If we manage to get a few pints home (without the berries being gobbled up in the backseat), I dip the strawberries in homemade vanilla sugar for a simple treat.

KIDS CAN: Children can prepare and assemble this dessert in one of two ways: either slicing the berries, dividing them among dishes, and sprinkling with vanilla sugar; or simply dipping whole berries into a bowl of vanilla sugar to coat.

---

2 cups pure cane sugar

1 vanilla bean

1 pint strawberries

---

1. Pour the sugar into a large lidded glass jar. Slice the vanilla bean lengthwise and scrape the seeds into the sugar, then toss in the pod. Mix everything together. Let the jar of vanilla sugar sit on the counter for 1 to 2 weeks before using, allowing the vanilla flavor to soak into the sugar crystals.

2. To serve, simply dip whole strawberries into a small bowl of the vanilla sugar. Or, if you want something juicer, slice the berries, toss them with vanilla sugar, and set them aside at room temperature for 1 hour or until the sugar begins to dissolve and the strawberries look juicy.

FOR BABY: Babies can enjoy a pile of diced strawberries.

The Solons' Family Meal, West Tisbury, Massachusetts

HERBY PASTA WITH MUSSELS AND LEEKS

CAESAR-ISH SALAD WITH ROSEMARY CROUTONS

RHUBARB CAKE WITH VANILLA CRÈME FRAÎCHE

shared by Gina Solon

After long, bleak months of wet, frigid weather, the days start to stretch, sometimes warming up just for a bit—just enough to cast upon us a little hope. In our family, many spring afternoons are spent outside. There is much unearthing to do from the remains of autumn and winter in our sandboxes and tree houses and gardens. And at least once a day there is a walk to our family farm. Lambs are coming at full speed now, and at any moment there could be another; you just have to peek. I love winter food—rich, substantial dishes that take hours to make—but in the spring, I am ready for brighter, crisper things. This meal is a combination of fresh and vibrant flavors, quickly assembled but still warm and comforting. Perfect for the evenings when we roll into the house with cold fingertips, smelling like the earth.

HERBY PASTA WITH MUSSELS AND LEEKS

serves 6

I usually have most of the ingredients for the pasta dish lying around, except for the mussels, which are super affordable and readily available at most fish markets.

- 1 pound whole-wheat spaghetti
- 5 tablespoons olive oil
- 4 leeks, white and light green parts sliced into 1-inch pieces
- ¾ cup dry white wine
- 2 pounds mussels, scrubbed and rinsed clean
- 3 tablespoons unsalted butter
- ¼ cup chopped fresh flat-leaf parsley
- 1 tablespoon chopped fresh thyme
- 1 tablespoon chopped fresh chives
- Kosher salt
- Red pepper flakes

---

1. Bring a large pot of salted water to a boil. Cook the pasta until just al dente, according to the package instructions, then drain the pasta, reserving ½ cup of the starchy cooking liquid.
2. Heat the oil in a large sauté pan over medium heat and add the leeks. Cook for 3 to 4 minutes, stirring constantly, until the leeks are slightly translucent. Add the wine, the reserved pasta water, and the mussels. Cover the pan and cook for about 5 to 6 minutes, until the mussels open. (Discard any mussels that haven't opened after cooking.)
3. Add the butter, pasta, and herbs to the pan and cook, tossing constantly, for about 1 to 2 minutes more. Season with salt and a sprinkle of red pepper flakes.

FOR BABY: As shellfish is a top allergenic food, talk to your pediatrician before experimenting with mussels. Pasta tossed with olive oil, with or without mussels, can be finely chopped for a finger food.

CAESAR-ISH SALAD WITH ROSEMARY CROUTONS

serves 4 to 6

When he was nine years old, my husband went to a restaurant where they made Caesar salad tableside, and he's been making it at home ever since. This is our toned-down, family-friendly version. The salad is easy to throw together; the littles can tear the lettuce and mix the dressing all on their own. The croutons fill the house with a toasty, rosemary scent, and often half of them are gone before they make it into the bowl.

KIDS CAN: Little hands can tear lettuce leaves for the salad and mix together the dressing.

DRESSING

⅛ cup extra virgin olive oil

2 heaping tablespoons real mayonnaise

¼ cup buttermilk

1 garlic clove, grated

2 tablespoons freshly squeezed lemon juice

Big pinch kosher salt

A few grinds freshly ground black pepper

CROUTONS

½ loaf crusty bread, cut into 1-inch cubes

Leaves from 2 sprigs fresh rosemary

4 to 5 tablespoons unsalted butter

2 large heads romaine lettuce

Freshly grated Parmesan cheese

1. To make the dressing, whisk together the olive oil, mayonnaise, buttermilk, garlic, lemon juice, salt, and pepper in a medium bowl. Cover and chill in the fridge for at least 15 minutes.
2. To make the croutons, preheat the oven to 400°F. Spread the bread cubes on a large, rimmed baking sheet. With a mortar and pestle, grind the rosemary until the leaves are broken down and you have kind of a paste. In a small saucepan over medium-low heat, melt the butter. Add the rosemary and swirl it around a few times to flavor the butter. Drizzle the rosemary butter over the bread cubes and toss with a spatula to coat them on all sides. Transfer the baking sheet to the oven and bake the croutons for about 10 minutes, until toasty and golden.
3. To assemble the salad, tear the romaine heads into large pieces and place them in a large salad bowl. Drizzle the lettuce with the dressing and add the croutons. Grate some Parmesan on top and toss gently with tongs.

RHUBARB CAKE WITH VANILLA CRÈME FRAÎCHE

makes one 8 by 8-inch cake

I love to make this simple cake using the abundance of rhubarb from my mother-in-law's garden. It doubles as a breakfast cake in our house, too, often inhaled on the way to the bus stop.

---

1 cup whole-wheat flour

1 cup unbleached all-purpose flour

1 teaspoon baking soda

1 teaspoon kosher salt

½ cup (1 stick) unsalted butter, at room temperature

1½ cups packed dark brown sugar

2 large eggs, at room temperature

1½ teaspoons pure vanilla extract

1 cup plain full-fat yogurt, at room temperature

3 to 4 stalks fresh rhubarb, trimmed and cut into 1-inch pieces

1 tablespoon grated fresh gingerroot

VANILLA CRÈME FRAÎCHE

Seeds from 1 vanilla bean

One 8-ounce container crème fraîche

2 tablespoons confectioners' sugar

---

1. Grease an 8 by 8-inch baking dish and preheat the oven to 350°F.

2. In a large bowl, stir together the flours, baking soda, and salt. In the bowl of an electric mixer fitted with the paddle attachment, cream together the butter and sugar. Add the eggs and vanilla, beat well to combine, then alternate between the flour mixture and the yogurt, adding a little at a time and beating well between additions. When all the flour and yogurt has been incorporated, fold in the rhubarb and ginger with a wooden spoon or rubber spatula.

3. Pour the batter into the prepared baking dish and bake for about 55 minutes or until a knife inserted in the center comes out clean.

4. To make the crème fraîche topping, mix together all the ingredients in a small bowl. Cover and refrigerate for at least 15 minutes or until chilled. Top the cake slices with dollops of the crème fraîche.

FOR BABY: Rhubarb cake can be crumbled into bits for a special treat.

A Savory (and Very Green) Pie

SKILLET SPINACH PIE

PUFFED BROWN RICE TREATS

I grew up in a suburb of Boston. My hometown looks a lot different now than it did thirty years ago. Now, Main Street is lined with bustling restaurants, upscale stores, and fancy wine shops. Back in the day, we made our way between an ice cream shop, movie rental store, and Greek restaurant. This neighborhood Greek restaurant is where our family would go for a night out. I first saw moussaka, tasted egg-lemon soup, and bit into baklava sitting around its white-clothed tables. My order was always a slice of spinach pie, a dish I continue to love today. This meal is a simple, home-cooked version of the Greek classic, paired with my twist on another classic, crispy rice treats.

SKILLET SPINACH PIE

serves 8

Foolproof skillet meals are hard to beat, and this one is just as impressive as it is delicious. Don't be intimidated by the phyllo dough—an imperfect top will only result in more crisp edges. I often grill up a few local pork sausages to serve alongside this vegetable pie, but a big slice on its own is perfectly good, too.

KIDS CAN: Kids can wrap the cooked spinach in kitchen towels and squeeze out the moisture.

---

30 ounces frozen spinach, thawed
5 tablespoons unsalted butter
1 small yellow onion, minced
2 cups whole-milk ricotta cheese
4 large eggs, lightly beaten
⅓ cup crumbled feta cheese
3 tablespoons chopped fresh dill
Juice of 1 lemon
1 teaspoon kosher salt
Freshly ground black pepper
6 sheets frozen phyllo dough, thawed

---

1. Preheat the oven to 375°F.
2. Place the spinach in the center of a clean kitchen towel, then fold up the edges and squeeze out as much moisture as you can.
3. In a 10-inch cast iron (or other ovenproof) skillet, melt the butter over medium heat. Transfer 2 tablespoons of melted butter to a small bowl. Add the minced onion to the skillet and cook until softened, about 5 minutes. Turn off the heat and let the pan cool slightly, then stir in the spinach, ricotta, eggs, feta, dill, lemon juice, salt, and a few grinds of pepper.
4. Lay the first sheet of phyllo dough over the spinach-ricotta mixture in the skillet and brush the top with some of the reserved melted butter. One at a time, layer on the remaining five sheets, brushing each with butter. Rotate and scrunch each sheet slightly so the edges are offset and the top is ruffled. Transfer the pie to the oven and bake until golden brown and heated through, about 35 minutes.

FOR BABY: Spinach tends to be stringy, so whiz a serving of pie in a food processor to break up any long strands.

TOMORROW'S DINNER: This recipe makes a big pan of spinach pie, plenty for leftovers. Serve a quick Greek egg-lemon soup or pan of lamb meatballs with the leftovers.

PUFFED BROWN RICE TREATS

makes about 16 treats

If the kids are eager to help in the kitchen, we often choose to make these treats for dessert. The recipe can be completed by little helpers, start to finish, and takes only a few minutes to get from mixing bowl to mouth. This recipe makes a slightly sweet treat. If you like a stronger dose of sweetness, add in another tablespoon of maple syrup. Similarly, the treats are soft and squishy at first (they harden up on the counter). If you want a firm, crisp treat from the start, add in a bit more of the sticky stuff (brown rice syrup and nut butter).

---

5 cups puffed brown rice cereal
1 teaspoon coconut oil, melted
1 cup brown rice syrup
2 tablespoons almond butter (or any nut or seed butter)
2 tablespoons pure maple syrup
2 teaspoons pure vanilla extract

---

1. Pour the cereal into a large mixing bowl.
2. Place the coconut oil in a saucepan over medium-high heat. Add in the rice syrup, almond butter, and maple syrup. Stir to combine and heat until bubbles form. Let the mixture boil for 5 minutes, then immediately turn off the heat and stir in the vanilla extract.
3. Pour the syrup into the bowl with the cereal and mix well. Scrape the mixture into an 8 by 8-inch pan. With slightly wet hands, press the mixture flat. Let it cool to room temperature, then slice it into squares and serve. If your eaters are eager, you can dig in right away, but the bars will be lose. Leftover treats can be stored in an airtight container at room temperature for up to 1 week.

FOR BABY: If your baby is comfortable with nuts, pull a rice treat apart into small grains of finger food. If you are avoiding nuts, swap the almond butter for a seed butter instead.

For the Busiest Night

SLOW COOKER INDIAN BUTTER CHICKEN WITH SWEET PEAS

LEMON-PECAN SHORTBREAD COOKIES

If you need a complete make-ahead meal for one of those days when soccer runs until 5:30 P.M., you have a late meeting, or the temperature just hit sixty degrees for the first time so there is no way you are cooking inside, look no further. This is a favorite slow cooker meal that requires no initial cooking steps—just toss everything in the pot and dinner is ready eight hours later.

SLOW COOKER INDIAN BUTTER CHICKEN WITH SWEET PEAS

serves 4 to 6

I encourage you to make this meal your own by choosing toppings and sides that are your family's favorites or that need to be eaten up. You know the ones—like that last sprinkle of nuts taking up precious storage space and staring at you, longingly, from the cabinet. I typically boil up some rice and toast slivered almonds with a handful of flaked coconut, but warm naan bread is another good accompaniment.

KIDS CAN: Little hands can use child-safe knives or kitchen shears to chop cilantro for the garnish.

- 2 pounds boneless, skinless chicken pieces (thighs and/or breasts)
- 1 onion, finely chopped
- 6 garlic cloves, finely chopped
- 1-inch piece fresh gingerroot, peeled and finely chopped
- 2 teaspoons curry powder
- 1 teaspoon ground cinnamon
- 1 teaspoon ground cumin
- 1 teaspoon kosher salt
- 4 tablespoons unsalted butter, cut into pieces
- One 6-ounce jar tomato paste
- One 13.5-ounce can full-fat coconut milk
- 3 tablespoons plain full-fat Greek yogurt
- 2 tablespoons freshly squeezed lemon juice
- 1½ cups sweet peas (thawed if frozen or blanched if fresh)
- Cooked basmati rice, for serving

TOPPINGS (OPTIONAL)

- Chopped fresh cilantro
- Toasted coconut flakes
- Toasted slivered almonds

---

1. Cut the chicken into 2-inch chunks. Fill a 6-quart slow cooker with the chicken, onion, garlic, ginger, curry powder, cinnamon, cumin, and salt. Stir to combine. Add in the butter, tomato paste, and coconut milk. Mix again. Cover and cook on low for 8 hours until the chicken pulls apart easily with a fork.

2. Before serving, stir in the Greek yogurt, lemon juice, and peas. Allow everything to heat through, then serve the butter chicken over a bed of basmati rice. Top with cilantro, toasted coconut, and toasted slivered almonds, if desired.

FOR BABY: Indian Butter Chicken is very tender and can be easily shredded with two forks. Mix in some rice and you have baby's meal.

TOMORROW'S DINNER: NAAN ROLL-UPS

Toast a few pieces of naan bread, spread on a thin layer of mango chutney, then spoon some left-over butter chicken on top. Roll up the naan and serve with a big salad.

LEMON-PECAN SHORTBREAD COOKIES

makes 1 to 2 dozen cookies, depending on the size of your cutter

If you want a dessert that's just as hands-off as dinner, roll out a prepared disc of this Lemon-Pecan Shortbread Cookie dough (perhaps made over the weekend) and bake up a tray in just 10 minutes.

KIDS CAN: Everyone can help roll out and stamp the cookies for dessert.

1 cup unbleached all-purpose flour

1 cup whole-wheat pastry flour

⅓ cup pecans, chopped

1 tablespoon chia seeds

¼ teaspoon kosher salt

Zest of 2 lemons

1 cup (2 sticks) unsalted butter, at room temperature

½ cup coconut sugar

1. In a medium bowl, whisk together the flours, pecans, chia seeds, salt, and lemon zest. Set aside. In a separate bowl, or in the bowl of an electric mixer, beat the butter with the coconut sugar until smooth, about 1 minute. Add the flour mixture to the butter mixture and beat until just combined.
2. Shape the dough into a round, flat disk and wrap it tightly in plastic. Refrigerate the dough for at least 1 hour or overnight.
3. About 15 minutes before you're ready to stamp out your cookie shapes, remove the dough from the refrigerator and let it sit on the counter to soften up. Preheat the oven to 350°F and line a rimmed baking sheet with parchment paper.
4. Unwrap the dough and place it on a lightly floured work surface. Roll out the dough to a ¼-inch thickness and stamp it into your desired shapes using cookie cutters. Place the shapes on the prepared baking sheet and bake until the cookies are golden at the edges, 10 to 15 minutes, depending on the size of the cookies. Remove the baking sheet from the oven, let the cookies rest for 1 minute, then transfer them to a wire rack to cool completely. The cookies can be stored on the counter in an airtight container for up to 1 week.

FOR BABY: Older infants who are comfortable with nuts can hold a Lemon-Pecan Cookie and gnaw on dessert.

Rainy Spring Days Need Stew (and Bread)

CHICKPEA STEW WITH BROCCOLI PESTO

SIMPLE DUTCH OVEN BREAD

You know the old saying about March—in like a lion, out like a lamb? Well, this dinner is for those lion days when it is dark, wet, and sad. Afternoons like these often start with picking up wet and dripping kids at school. We race home, toss all the soggy clothes in the dryer, put on pajamas, and sit (or zoom around on scooters) on the front porch watching the rain fall. When the crew is ready, we head in, fill big bowls with stew, rip off chunks of bread, and head back out to huddle under the overhangs, watch the storm, and slurp it all up.

CHICKPEA STEW WITH BROCCOLI PESTO

serves 6 to 8

Our kids are less suspicious of vegetables that are in soups and stews, so that is where I pack them in the most. I have found it important to finely chop the root vegetables, with the help of a food processor, and take time slicing the Swiss chard into fine ribbons. If a stew is hard for my guys to eat, then they get turned off quickly. The broccoli pesto topping is an added bonus of flavor and nutrition.

KIDS CAN: Kitchen helpers can wash the Swiss chard, tear the leaves from the stems, and then rip the leaves into small pieces.

---

3 tablespoons olive oil

3 to 4 medium carrots, peeled and cut into large chunks

4 to 5 celery ribs, cut into large chunks

3 to 4 shallots, peeled

2 garlic cloves

Two 15-ounce cans chickpeas, drained and rinsed

4 cups low-sodium chicken broth

One 8-ounce can pureed tomatoes

1½ teaspoons kosher salt

Freshly ground black pepper

3 sprigs fresh thyme

1 bay leaf

5 Swiss chard leaves, thick stems removed, cut into fine ribbons

Juice of 1 lemon

Broccoli Pesto (recipe follows)

---

1. Warm the olive oil in a soup pot set over medium heat. While the pot warms, whiz the carrots, celery, shallots, and garlic in a food processor to form a fine paste. Add the vegetable mixture to the pot and sauté for 10 minutes, until soft.

2. Add the chickpeas, broth, tomatoes, salt, a few grinds of black pepper, the thyme, and the bay leaf to the pot. Bring the stew to a boil. Reduce the heat to medium-low and simmer for 20 minutes, until the vegetables are very soft and the broth is slightly thickened.

3. Add the chard ribbons to the stew and cook for 10 minutes more. Before serving, remove the thyme sprigs and bay leaf, then squirt in the lemon juice. Serve the stew with dollops of broccoli pesto and crusty bread.

FOR BABY: For young infants, puree or smash a small bowl of stew to create a smooth and creamy consistency.

BROCCOLI PESTO

makes about 2 cups

This is a versatile, nutrient-packed condiment to have on hand. It tastes best warm, tossed with pasta, folded into scrambled eggs, or stirred into boiled potatoes.

KIDS CAN: Older children can whiz all the broccoli pesto ingredients together.

---

2 cups bite-size broccoli florets
2 small or 1 large garlic clove
1 lightly packed cup fresh basil leaves
⅓ cup extra virgin olive oil
½ cup grated Romano cheese
Squirt of freshly squeezed lemon juice
Kosher salt, to taste

---

1. Steam the broccoli florets in a steamer basket set atop a pot of boiling water for about 7 minutes or until just fork-tender, not mushy. Drain well.
2. In the bowl of a food processor, combine the steamed broccoli, garlic, basil, olive oil, cheese, lemon juice, and a big pinch of salt. Whiz until everything is combined. Taste for salt and add more if needed. Extra broccoli pesto can be stored in an airtight container in the refrigerator for a few days. It is best eaten warm or at room temperature.

SIMPLE DUTCH OVEN BREAD

makes 1 round loaf

In my opinion, fresh, warm bread is a necessary accompaniment to the soup pot. Here, I'm sharing our no-knead Dutch oven loaf that requires almost no attention, but does take time.

---

2 cups whole wheat flour
2 cups bread flour
2 teaspoons kosher salt
¾ teaspoon active dry yeast
2 cups warm water

---

1. In a big bowl, mix together the flours, salt, and yeast. Pour the warm water into the bowl and, using a wooden spoon, mix again until the water is incorporated. Cover the bowl tightly with plastic wrap and let it sit on the counter for 12 to 18 hours.

2. When you're ready to bake the bread, preheat the oven to 475°F and set a rack in the middle of the oven. (If your rack and pot are too close to the heating element, the bottom of the bread will burn.) Preheat a Dutch oven in the hot oven for 10 minutes. When your pot is ready, lightly flour your hands, gently remove the dough from the bowl, and roughly shape it into a ball. Drop the ball of dough into the pot. Cover the pot with the lid and place it back in the oven. Bake the bread for 30 minutes with the lid on, then remove the lid and bake for another 10 to 15 minutes, until golden brown. Remove from the oven and let cool.

FOR BABY: If the bread is too crusty for your little one, drop small bread balls into the soup broth to soften up.

TOMORROW'S DINNER: OPEN-FACED GRILLED CHEESE SANDWICHES

Top slices of the bread with broccoli pesto, turkey breast, sliced tomato, and cheddar cheese. Lay the sandwiches on a baking sheet and broil in the oven until the cheese is melted and golden brown. Serve with fruit salad.

Magic Word—"Noodles!"

SESAME NOODLES WITH BOK CHOY AND SWEET PEPPERS

CILANTRO-LIME GRILLED TUNA

You will find these sesame noodles on our dinner table at least once a week, all year round. When Dylan asks, "What's for dinner?" and I answer, "The brown noodles," he does a celebratory jump. Meals that elicit celebratory jumps should be served weekly, as far as I am concerned. You can sauté any vegetables you like to toss in with the noodles, but bok choy and sweet peppers are my favorite because they're colorful and quick to cook. These noodles are delicious topped with a skewer of grilled fish, but anything you feel like swapping in (chicken or beef) will be just as tasty basted with cilantro-lime marinade and cooked over hot flames.

SESAME NOODLES WITH BOK CHOY AND SWEET PEPPERS

serves 4 to 6

Over the years I have been gifted many a bok choy bunch. Friends often receive loads of the Chinese cabbage in their CSA boxes and are unsure how to prepare it. My favorite technique is shared here: thinly sliced and sautéed in a hot pan. As sesame noodles are such a crowd pleaser at our house, they make a good base when experimenting with new and surprising vegetables. Leftover sesame noodles are our family's favorite packed lunch: they are still delicious at room temperature and follow the "no-nuts" school rule. When I go to pack lunches at 6 A.M. and find the leftovers ready to go, I do my own happy dance.

KIDS CAN: Helpers can chop the bok choy and bell pepper with child-safe knives or kitchen shears. Kids can also whisk together the sauce and sprinkle on the sesame seeds.

Two 8.8-ounce packages soba noodles

2 tablespoons canola oil, divided

2 bunches bok choy, trimmed and sliced into thin ribbons

1 red, yellow, or orange bell pepper, thinly sliced

¼ cup soy sauce

1 tablespoon honey

2 garlic cloves, shaved on a microplane

1½-inch piece fresh gingerroot, peeled and shaved on a microplane

2 tablespoons rice vinegar

1 tablespoon toasted sesame oil

4 scallions, white and light green parts only, thinly sliced

Cilantro-Lime Grilled Tuna (recipe follows)

TOPPINGS (OPTIONAL)

Sesame seeds

Sriracha sauce

---

1. Bring a big pot of water to a boil. Boil the soba noodles for 5 minutes or until tender, then drain them and set aside.

2. While you wait for the water to boil, heat 1 tablespoon of the canola oil in a medium sauté pan set over medium-high heat. Cook the bok choy and pepper, stirring constantly, until wilted and slightly charred, 5 to 7 minutes. Turn off the heat.

3. In a large bowl, whisk together the soy sauce, honey, garlic, ginger, rice vinegar, sesame oil, and the remaining 1 tablespoon of canola oil. Add the warm noodles to the bowl and toss well. Top the noodles with the vegetables, sliced scallions, and sesame seeds, if using. Serve with sriracha sauce and Cilantro-Lime Grilled Tuna.

FOR BABY: Using kitchen shears or a food processor, chop up a bowl of noodles for baby to enjoy.

TOMORROW'S DINNER: Miso Soba Soup—Heat 1 quart of vegetable stock and whisk in 6 tablespoons of miso paste. Cut a block of extra-firm tofu into small cubes. Add the leftover noodles and cubed tofu to the broth. Let everything heat through before serving.

CILANTRO-LIME GRILLED TUNA

serves 4 to 6

I have grilled up a variety of fish and meat to top sesame noodles—everything from tuna to chicken and beef—and this simple cilantro-lime marinade goes great with them all. On more leisurely evenings we grill outside, but a simple grill pan on the stovetop does a fine job on those hectic nights.

KIDS CAN: For those who like touching squishy things, skewering up the fish is a fun job.

¼ cup extra virgin olive oil

3 tablespoons chopped fresh cilantro (if you're not a big fan of cilantro, fresh basil works well, too)

Juice of 2 limes

Kosher salt and freshly ground black pepper

1½ pounds sushi-grade tuna, cut into 1-inch cubes

4 to 6 wooden skewers, soaked in water for at least 10 minutes

---

1. In a shallow dish, whisk together the oil, cilantro, lime juice, a big pinch of salt, and a few grinds of black pepper. Add in the tuna cubes and toss gently to coat the fish on all sides. Cover the dish with plastic wrap and refrigerate for at least 30 minutes or up to 1 hour. You don't want to leave the tuna in the marinade too long, as the acid in the lime juice will start to cook the fish.

2. When you're ready to cook, heat a grill or grill pan to medium-high and lightly oil the grates. Fill a shallow baking dish with water and soak the wooden skewers (if using) for at least 10 minutes. To assemble the skewers, working with one at a time, push the skewer's tip through the middle of a marinated fish cube. Repeat, tightly packing skewers with fish. Assemble 4 skewers of fish. Reserve the remaining marinade in the container. Put the skewers on the grill and brush them with some of the reserved marinade. Grill the skewers for 2 minutes, then flip them, brush them with more marinade, and grill for another 2 minutes. The outside of the fish should have deep grill marks, while the inside should still be pink and rare. Remove the skewers from the heat and brush them one last time with more of the reserved marinade, then serve.

FOR BABY: Tuna can be high in mercury, so be mindful of your child's intake. Cut the tuna into small pieces for baby to enjoy.

A Plate of Spring Colors

RED LENTILS WITH COCONUT MILK AND SPINACH

BLACK RICE WITH DRIED PEACHES AND ALMONDS

CHOCOLATE-MINT MILKSHAKES

I first developed this dinner when our oldest son began eating table food. I was tired of making cubes of baby purees and knew there had to be nutritionally dense dishes that we could all enjoy. These Red Lentils with Coconut Milk and Spinach offer a soft texture and powerful mix of protein, healthy fat, and vitamins, making a perfect meal for both the oldest and youngest family member. These days, I serve this recipe to slightly more grown-up–looking baby faces, with black rice (because the kids think it's cool) tossed with dried peaches and toasted almonds. It is a rainbow plate of pink, green, and coral colors that always leaves me feeling light, refreshed, and content. An equally refreshing two-minute milkshake is the grand finale.

RED LENTILS WITH COCONUT MILK AND SPINACH

serves 4

Many parents want to offer a variety of beans and lentils to their children but are worried about problems with gas, cramping, bloating, or indigestion. Every body is different and reacts to legumes in its own way. Keep in mind that, in general, smaller lentils are easier to digest than large beans. For young eaters, this simple recipe of red lentils stewed in coconut milk is a good place to start.

KIDS CAN: This dinner has a lot of colorful ingredients with interesting textures. Make a small tray of dried red lentils, black forbidden rice, sliced almonds, cocoa powder, and mint leaves for your kids to touch and explore.

---

2 tablespoons olive oil
2 cups red lentils
Two 14-ounce cans coconut milk
1 cup water
1-inch piece fresh gingerroot, peeled
1 teaspoon kosher salt
2 packed cups baby spinach, roughly chopped

---

1. Warm the olive oil in a saucepan set over medium heat. Add the lentils to the pan and toast for 1 minute. After 1 minute, add in the coconut milk, water, ginger, and salt. Cover the pan with a lid and simmer over low heat until the lentils are tender and the liquid is almost fully absorbed, about 20 minutes.
2. When you're ready to eat, remove the ginger, stir in the spinach leaves, and cook just until the spinach has wilted. Taste for salt and serve warm.

FOR BABY: Red Lentils with Coconut Milk and Spinach is an ideal dinner for baby, as it is packed with healthy fats, protein, and fiber. For young eaters, overcook the lentils slightly so they fall apart and lose any hard bite. Then, stir in finely chopped baby spinach.

BLACK RICE WITH DRIED PEACHES AND ALMONDS

serves 4

I like adding dried fruit (for sweetness) and toasted nuts (for a salty crunch) to rice sides. Here, anything from apricots to raisins, walnuts to pistachios, will do. Put your kids in charge of picking out a couple of additions from the pantry to add to the rice.

---

1 cup black forbidden rice
½ cup dried peaches, diced
½ cup sliced almonds, toasted
3 tablespoons extra virgin olive oil
½ teaspoon kosher salt

---

1. Boil the rice in a large pot of salted water until tender, about 20 minutes.
2. While the rice cooks, toss together the dried peaches, almonds, olive oil, and salt in a large serving bowl. Drain the rice, toss to remove any excess liquid, add it to the bowl with the dried peaches and almonds. Mix well before serving.

CHOCOLATE-MINT MILKSHAKES

makes 4 milkshakes

It's so much fun to say yes to a chocolate milkshake for dessert (especially if you live with a chocoholic like I do), so why not try this wholesome version, naturally sweetened with dates and frozen banana. Our sad excuse for a back garden does continuously produce fragrant mint, allowing the boys to run out, grab a few sprigs, and return bringing that sweet scent with them.

---

5 dates, pitted

2 cups whole milk (or your favorite unsweetened nut or plant milk)

3 tablespoons unsweetened cocoa powder

1 cup ice

1 frozen banana

5 fresh mint leaves

---

1. Simply whiz everything together in a blender, divide among 4 glasses, and enjoy immediately.

Spring Sunday Supper

SPLAYED ROAST CHICKEN WITH SPRING VEGETABLES

LEMON-RED BULGUR SALAD

SMASHED POTATOES

STRAWBERRY-ORANGE SLAB PIE

For Mother's Day this year, we invited my parents, sister, and brother-in-law over for a celebratory Sunday supper. I made a splayed roast chicken surrounded by leeks, asparagus, and scallions, based on a recipe shared by an old friend. To soak up the chicken drippings, I added a quick red bulgur salad to the table, along with smashed roasted potatoes (because no party is a real party without crispy potatoes). The meal was finished off with a rustic Strawberry-Orange Slab Pie. The dinner was so good that I scribbled it down a few hours later, vowing to re-create it again soon. Since then, we have eaten this meal a dozen times, always toasting to something, from the last day of school to a new job.

SPLAYED ROAST CHICKEN WITH SPRING VEGETABLES

serves 4 to 6

You should make this dinner on the first warm evening in spring, and here is how: Pop the cast iron skillet in the oven to warm up. Everything else can be prepared in just ten minutes. Now, go outside. Take a quick walk, dust off your bike, push your baby on the swing. If your kids want to help, have them snap the asparagus, or (if your children are anything like ours) inquire about the details of the dead chicken (Where are its feathers? Did it have a head?). Forty minutes later, come back to the kitchen, put the chicken in the oven, and remind the kids that you have Strawberry-Orange Slab Pie for dessert—they will be psyched.

One 4- to 5-pound chicken
2 teaspoons kosher salt
6 grinds black pepper
1 lemon, quartered
1 leek
1 bunch asparagus
3 tablespoons extra virgin olive oil
5 garlic cloves, smashed and peeled
6 scallions

---

1. Place a large cast iron (or other heavy ovenproof) skillet in the oven and preheat to 500°F. Leave the pan in the oven for 45 minutes as the oven gets to temperature. (If your oven is dirty it will smoke, so look it over before cranking up the heat.)
2. While the oven and pan preheat, place the chicken on a cutting board and season it all over with the salt and pepper. Using a sharp knife, cut the skin connecting the legs to the body. Splay the thighs open until you feel the joint pop on each side, then place 2 of the lemon wedges inside the chicken. Set aside.
3. Prep the leeks by first trimming off the rough dark green top and root bottom. Slice the white and light green part in half vertically and then into thin half rounds. Rinse the sliced leeks in a large pot of water to remove the trapped dirt. Drain.
4. Prep the asparagus by trimming the ends and slicing the stalks vertically into thin sticks.
5. Prep the scallions by trimming the root ends and dark green parts, and slicing in half vertically.
6. When the pan is ready, carefully remove it from the oven and pour in 1 tablespoon of the oil. Transfer the chicken, breast-side up, to the hot skillet. Drizzle the bird with another tablespoon of the oil. Roast for 30 minutes. After 30 minutes, toss in all the veggies (you'll have to

(continued)

use a spatula to squish everything in around the bird), the two remaining lemon quarters, and another tablespoon of oil. Roast for 5 minutes more, then stir again. Continue roasting for 10 more minutes, until the vegetables are soft and the skin is golden. Remove the pan from the oven and let the chicken rest for 5 minutes, then carve and serve with the pan juices and vegetables.

FOR BABY: Finely chop a serving of chicken and vegetables, using either a food processor or a sharp knife.

TOMORROW'S DINNER: CHEF'S SALAD

Roughly shop any leftover chicken, green vegetables, and potatoes. Toss these ingredients with baby greens, leftover cooked bulgur, hard-boiled eggs, and pieces of hard cheese (like Parmesan or cheddar). Dress the salad with lemon-mustard vinaigrette and serve with crusty bread.

LEMON-RED BULGUR SALAD

serves 4

A staple in Middle Eastern and Mediterranean regions, bulgur is a wonderful and versatile ingredient. Red bulgur is whole-grain hard red wheat that has been parboiled, dried, and cracked. I find it in the bulk bin section of our market. Red bulgur is quick to cook, and the result is a fiber-rich side that is both fluffy and chewy. Here, I drizzle on some lemon butter, toss, and serve warm.

1 cup red bulgur
2 cups water
3 tablespoons unsalted butter
Zest of 1 lemon
Minced fresh chives or parsley, for serving (optional)

1. Combine the bulgur and water in a small saucepan over high heat. Bring the water to a boil, then cover the pan, reduce the heat to low, and simmer for 15 to 20 minutes, until all the liquid is absorbed. Meanwhile, melt the butter with the lemon zest in another small saucepan. Pour the lemon butter over the cooked bulgur, add the salt, and fluff with a fork. Top with minced fresh chives or parsley, if you like.

FOR BABY: The bulgur is soft and small—a nice finger food for baby.

SMASHED POTATOES

serves 4 to 6

As someone who would be perfectly happy eating French fries for most meals, I can tell you that these smashed potatoes are just as good. Small potatoes are parboiled, flattened, and then roasted until crispy. If you love salt and vinegar potato chips, sprinkle a bit of malt vinegar over the potatoes before putting them in the oven. They are addictive; you've been warned.

KIDS CAN: Smashing the potatoes is a fun, active job for little helpers.

Kosher salt

2 pounds small red potatoes

3 tablespoons olive oil, divided

1. Preheat the oven to 450°F.
2. While the oven warms, bring a large pot of salted water to a boil over high heat. Add the potatoes and boil them for 10 minutes or until fork-tender. Drain the potatoes and let them cool for 10 minutes.
3. Brush a rimmed baking sheet with 1 tablespoon of the olive oil. Using the back of a heavy pan or the bottom of a strong cup, smash each potato into a flat pancake and lay it on the oiled pan. Brush the tops of the smashed potatoes with the remaining 2 tablespoons of oil and sprinkle them evenly with salt. Transfer the potatoes to the oven. Roast for 10 minutes, flip each potato, sprinkle them again with salt, and roast for 10 minutes more or until crisp and golden.

STRAWBERRY-ORANGE SLAB PIE

makes one 9 by 13-inch pie

Slab pie gives regular old circular pie a run for its money. First, there is a higher crust-to-filling ratio . . . and pie crust is everything. Slab pies can also feed a lot more people—or, they allow you to get a second (and third) slice.

DOUGH

- 2 cups unbleached all-purpose flour, plus more for dusting
- ½ teaspoon kosher salt
- 1 cup (2 sticks) cold unsalted butter, cut into ½-inch cubes
- ¼ cup ice water

FILLING

- 1½ pounds strawberries, hulled and quartered
- Zest of 1 orange
- ¼ cup honey
- 3 tablespoons unbleached all-purpose flour

- 1 large egg
- 2 tablespoons turbinado sugar
- Whipped cream, for serving (optional)
- Vanilla ice cream, for serving (optional)

1. To make the dough, place the flour and salt in the bowl of a food processor and pulse a few times to combine. Add the butter. Pulse 20 times or until the butter is the size of tiny pebbles. With the motor running, stream in the ice water and pulse until the dough pulls away from the sides of the bowl and begins to form a ball. Turn the mixture out onto a lightly floured counter and knead it to form a ball of dough. Divide the dough in half, shape each half into a 1-inch-thick disk, wrap each disk tightly with plastic, and refrigerate for at least 1 hour or up to 2 days.
2. When you are ready to assemble the pie, preheat the oven to 350°F. Remove your dough disks from the refrigerator and let them warm on the counter for 10 minutes.
3. To make the filling, in a medium bowl, gently mix the strawberries with the orange zest, honey, and flour.
4. Roll the first disk of dough into a rough rectangle to fit a 9 by 13-inch baking pan. Place the first rolled dough in the bottom of the pan. Roll out the second disk of dough for the top of the pie and set it aside.
5. Scoop the filling onto the rolled-out dough in the baking pan and spread it out evenly. Place the second sheet of dough on top of the filling and crimp the sides to seal (you can do this with your fingers or with a fork). Whisk the egg in a small bowl and brush it over the top of the pie. Cut a few slits in the top crust and sprinkle with the turbinado sugar. Bake for 45 to 50 minutes, until the top of the pie is golden brown. Serve with whipped cream or vanilla ice cream if you wish.

3

Summer

From spontaneously packed beach picnics to planned cookouts for ten friends, summer dinners should be about enjoying the extended daylight and not being stuck in a hot kitchen. I have been hugely pregnant two of the last four summers, so I have developed a host of fast and nutritious dinners that lessen the humid-grump factor of which I am a victim. Eating low-effort dinners like Slow Cooker Greek Chicken Gyros (page 204) and sweet desserts like Coconut, Chocolate, Cherry Pops (page 165) in a bathing suit is pretty much the best it gets. I often start our summer dinners with a platter of raw fruits and vegetables—tomatoes, cucumbers, green beans, peppers, melons, and berries. The sneaky mom trick is to serve them with toothpicks or large skewers for the kids to eat with. You want to stab that tomato while making a loud, somewhat barbaric screeching noise before gobbling it up? Go for it. And let's not forget the magnificent grill—the answer to almost any summer dinner dilemma and the beacon that draws all members of the family into the cooking process. We grill the classics, of course, but some of my favorite dishes also include grilled stone fruits and flatbreads topped with fresh basil pesto and vegetables. Like many parts of our summer dinners, the veggie toppings on our flatbreads are usually raw. Including cool and refreshing raw foods at dinnertime not only lessens the prep and cooking involved but also supports your body's hydration, digestion, energy levels, and overall health.

Summer Meals

Blue Plate Special

DINER-STYLE SMASHED BEEF BURGERS

EDAMAME SUCCOTASH

This classic American hamburger dinner may completely change the way your family approaches burger night. You know the quintessential diner burger—thin, crispy edges, and full of flavor? Well, this is it—and it can be made in your own kitchen in under ten minutes. Our burger night changed last year after I caught Nick reading up on how to create a perfect diner burger at home. This was good news for all of us, because once he catches the bug of wanting to master a specific cooking technique (see pizza crust, homemade pasta, and corn tortillas in this book), he dives in and doesn't let up until he is completely satisfied. Here, Nick shares what he learned and how you can turn a stressful Tuesday into a fun burger night.

DINER-STYLE SMASHED BEEF BURGERS

makes 4 burgers

In place of a large, flat-top grill for cooking, we use a well-seasoned cast iron skillet, and it works perfectly. The smash burger cooking process is a show, one worth gathering around to watch.

SAUCE

6 to 8 Quick Pickled Cucumbers (page 191)

¾ cup ketchup

¼ cup real mayonnaise

BURGERS

1 pound local ground beef

1 teaspoon canola oil

Kosher salt

Freshly ground black pepper

4 slices cheddar cheese (optional)

4 potato rolls, split (we like Martin's)

Bibb lettuce leaves, for serving (optional)

Sliced tomato, for serving (optional)

1. First, make the sauce. Chop the pickles into small pieces. Place them in a small bowl, add the ketchup and mayonnaise, and mix everything together and set aside.
2. To make the burgers, divide the beef into 4 equal-size portions and gently form each into a loose ball. It's important to be delicate and not to pack the meat too tight. Preheat a 10-inch cast iron skillet over high heat until smoking. Add the canola oil to the skillet and spread it around with a paper towel, taking away as much as possible.
3. Season the top of the balls of beef liberally with salt and pepper. Take the first ball and put it salted-side down onto the super-hot skillet. Immediately take a large, flat spatula and SMASH (not violently, just hard) the burger into a round, ¼-inch-thick patty. After about 2 minutes, flip the patty. It should have a dark, caramelized crust. Add a slice of cheese, if you like, and let it cook for another 30 seconds on the second side. Remove the burger from the pan. Repeat this process with the remaining 3 balls of meat.
4. Toast the potato rolls, place a burger in each one, slather the buns with sauce, and add any desired toppings. We like a light lettuce such as Bibb and thinly cut tomatoes.

FOR BABY: Crumble small bites of beef for baby to eat.

EDAMAME SUCCOTASH

serves 6

This quick succotash recipe balances out the richness of the burgers. I've replaced the traditional lima beans with edamame, an ingredient kids are becoming more and more familiar with.

KIDS CAN: Popping the edamame out of the pods is an ideal job for eager helpers (just be prepared to have beans all over your kitchen!). Kids can also shuck the corn, halve the tomatoes (with child-safe knives), and tear the basil.

- 2 tablespoons olive oil
- 1 small onion, chopped
- 1 garlic clove, minced
- 1½ cups halved cherry tomatoes (or 2 large tomatoes, roughly chopped)
- Kernels from 4 ears of corn
- 1 cup cooked edamame (thawed if frozen)
- 1 tablespoon apple cider vinegar
- 1 teaspoon kosher salt
- 6 grinds of black pepper
- ¼ cup sliced or torn fresh basil leaves

---

1. In a large skillet, warm the olive oil over medium heat. Add the onion and cook until softened, about 5 minutes, then add in the garlic and cook for another minute more, stirring constantly. Add the tomatoes, corn kernels, edamame, vinegar, salt, and pepper and cook, stirring often, until the tomatoes just begin to soften, about 5 minutes. Season to taste with more salt and pepper. Just before serving, stir in the basil and taste. Adjust the seasonings if needed.

FOR BABY: Puree a bit of succotash in a food processor for spoon-feeding younger infants. Older infants can feed themselves bits of the vegetables.

TOMORROW'S DINNER: SUMMER GRAIN SALAD

Cook a pot of your favorite grain (such as farro, brown rice, or quinoa) and toss it with leftover succotash. Grill up some fish or chicken to serve alongside.

Make Your Own Dinner

GRILLED FLATBREAD BAR

WHOLE ARTICHOKES

COCONUT, CHOCOLATE, CHERRY POPS

In the summer months, our family congregates at my parents' house almost every weekend to eat outdoor dinners together. Wanting to pull together a festive family pizza night, we struggled with a way to bake the pies without overheating the entire house (nobody wants to be near a 500-degree oven in August!). After a group brainstorming session, we experimented by brushing small disks of pizza dough with olive oil, tossing them on the outdoor grill, and then topping the flatbreads with our favorite spreads and raw veggie toppings. Success! Now this is a meal we make together weekly, always with a different crowd and a different item included in the topping lineup. Alongside the flatbreads, we boil up a pot of whole artichokes, then gather around a big table to peel the leaves and dunk them into melted butter. After the dishes are clear, it's Coconut, Chocolate, Cherry Pops for everyone (grown-ups included).

GRILLED FLATBREAD BAR

serves 4

This meal looks festive and fancy on the table, and it's a great way to use up any garden vegetables, half jars of sauces, or small hunks of cheese lying around. The pizza dough can be store-bought or homemade (page 22). As with any great topping-focused meal, the goal here is to let everyone create the flatbread of their dreams. Yes, sometimes my kids just eat grilled pizza dough and pass on all the colorful vegetable additions, but such is life.

KIDS CAN: Kids can knead and divide the pizza dough into four disks, then assemble their own individual flatbreads.

FLATBREADS

One 1-pound ball pizza dough, at room temperature

2 tablespoons olive oil, plus more for drizzling

TOPPINGS

1 cup cherry tomatoes, sliced

1 cup white mushrooms, cleaned and shaved with a mandoline

4 tablespoons crumbled goat cheese

4 tablespoons basil pesto

2 cups loosely packed baby arugula

Juice of 1 lemon or 3 tablespoons balsamic vinegar

Kosher salt and freshly ground black pepper

---

1. Heat the grill to medium high.
2. Divide the dough into 4 equal balls. Knead and stretch the dough into 4 rounds about ½-inch thick. Brush on both sides with the oil. Transfer the oiled dough to the grill. Grill the flatbreads until they are just puffed with visible grill marks on the bottom, then flip them and repeat on the second side. Each side will cook in less than 5 minutes.
3. Arrange the flatbread spreads and toppings on a table and let everyone build their own. The secret is to finish the assembled flatbreads with a squirt of fresh lemon juice or balsamic vinegar, a drizzle of olive oil, and some salt and pepper.

FOR BABY: Older infants can nibble on small cubes of pizza, while younger babies can snack on any appropriate finely chopped toppings.

TOMORROW'S DINNER: SUMMER PASTA SALAD

Boil 1 pound of whole wheat pasta and toss it with any leftover flatbread toppings. Toast up a handful of pine nuts for a crunchy garnish.

WHOLE ARTICHOKES

serves 4

When I was growing up, my mom often boiled pots of whole artichokes and set small ramekins of butter on the table for us to dive into. I know the process (and the spiny vegetable itself) is intimidating to some, but once you give it a shot you will see how simple it all is. This is definitely a dish to be eaten outdoors, as the scraped leaves, butter drips, and other bits end up leaving a trail, but I love a meal that forces us to roll up our sleeves and head outside.

4 whole fresh artichokes
1 lemon, quartered
1 small bunch fresh thyme
1 bay leaf
1 small bunch fresh chives
½ cup (1 stick) unsalted butter, melted, for dipping

1. Prepare each artichoke by trimming off the bottom of the stem and peeling away any thick leaves near the stem. Next, cut 1 inch off the top of the artichoke (this is the prickliest part) and, using kitchen shears, snip off the sharp thorns on each exterior leaf.
2. Place the prepared artichokes, lemon quarters, and herbs in a large pot. Cover with water, cover the pot, and bring to a boil over high heat. Uncover, and boil the artichokes for 25 to 30 minutes or until the tops of the stems are easily pierced with a knife. Drain the artichokes, sprinkle them with salt, and serve warm with melted butter for dipping.
3. How do you eat an artichoke? Simply peel away the leaves and dip the round bottom of each leaf into the melted butter. Scrape off the flesh from each leaf with your teeth. The center (or choke) of an artichoke is filled with small white and purple strands. Using a spoon, scoop the strands out and eat the entire choke, dipped in butter.

COCONUT, CHOCOLATE, CHERRY POPS

makes 10 to 12 pops

Pull out a tray of these frozen pops for dessert and let the kids run around the yard with them while the adults sit and sip cold beers—win, win.

Two 13.5-ounce cans full-fat coconut milk, divided

⅓ cup unsweetened cocoa powder

5 tablespoons agave nectar, divided

½ teaspoon pure vanilla extract

¾ cup fresh sweet cherries, pitted

Juice of ½ lemon

---

1. Pour 1 can of the coconut milk in a small mixing bowl. Whisk in the cocoa and 3 tablespoons of the agave nectar. In a separate bowl, mix the other can of coconut milk with the vanilla and the remaining 2 tablespoons of agave nectar. Finally, in a third bowl, smash the cherries and lemon juice together with the back of a fork to form a chunky sauce.

2. To assemble the pops, fill 10 to 12 ice pop molds one-third of the way with the vanilla mixture, then add a spoonful of mashed cherries. To finish, slowly top each pop with the chocolate coconut milk. Insert the ice pop sticks into the molds and freeze until set, at least 2 hours.

FOR BABY: For those old enough to hold them, Coconut, Chocolate, Cherry Pops are a sweet and special treat.

Not-Boring Chicken and Potatoes

CRISPY SEED AND NUT-CRUSTED CHICKEN

TOMATO-AVOCADO SALAD

SWEET AND SOUR POTATO SALAD

In many people's minds, dinner still means chicken and potatoes. Maybe it's the mass appeal, straightforward ingredients, or confidence in tried and true recipes that brings us back to this classic combo time after time. I completely understand the draw and find the pair popping up in many of our meals, too. That said, let's shake it up a bit while holding on to the things that we love about a chicken-and-potato dinner. Here, I'm suggesting flavorful, protein-packed crusted chicken topped with a raw, bright salad (no cooking required there). Add a scoop of potato salad on the side and you have a fresh take on classic, comforting summer food.

CRISPY SEED AND NUT-CRUSTED CHICKEN

serves 4

I know I'm going to get some eye rolls here by suggesting that you make your own bread crumbs with nuts and seeds, but trust me on this one. It takes two minutes to toss a few slices of bread, sesame seeds, and almonds into a food processor. This coating gives the chicken cutlets a thick, crispy crust full of flavor and added nutrition. If it's a hit with your family, whiz up a couple of batches of seed-and-nut bread crumbs and store them in an airtight glass jar in your pantry for future meals.

KIDS CAN: Older children can pound out the chicken.

---

4 slices sprouted wheat bread, toasted

¼ cup raw, unsalted sesame seeds

¼ cup raw, unsalted almonds

4 boneless, skinless chicken breasts

1 cup unbleached all-purpose flour

1 teaspoon kosher salt

2 large eggs

Canola oil, for frying

Tomato-Avocado Salad (recipe follows)

---

1. Whiz the bread, seeds, and almonds in a food processor to make fine crumbs. Transfer the bread crumb mixture to a large, shallow dish.
2. Using a meat pounder, rolling pin, or small skillet, pound each chicken breast to a ¼-inch thickness.
3. When you're ready to cook the chicken, set a wire rack on a rimmed baking sheet. Combine the flour and salt in a large, shallow dish. Place the eggs in another large, shallow dish and beat them with 2 tablespoons of water. Coat one chicken cutlet in flour, shaking off any excess. Transfer the floured chicken to the egg wash and turn it to coat, letting any excess run off. Finally, coat the chicken in the bread crumbs on both sides, pressing lightly to ensure that the bread crumbs adhere. Place the breaded chicken on the wire rack. Repeat with the remaining chicken, then sprinkle the coated chicken with a bit more salt.
4. Coat a 10-inch cast iron or other heavy skillet with a thin layer of canola oil and place it over medium-high heat. Allow the oil to heat up for a few minutes. Fry the chicken for 2 to 3 minutes per side, until golden. My large skillet comfortably fits 2 breasts at a time. When in doubt, work in batches, as you don't want to overcrowd the pan. Place the cooked chicken on a paper towel–lined tray to drain. Repeat with the remaining coated chicken pieces. Serve warm, topped with the Tomato-Avocado Salad.

FOR BABY: If your baby has yet to enjoy nuts, simply cut a strip of chicken, dredge it in flour and egg, and fry it alongside the crusted pieces. Serve chicken with smashed avocado and undressed potato.

TOMORROW'S DINNER: CHICKEN CUTLET SANDWICHES

Slice a hearty loaf of wheat bread and layer on leftover chicken, smashed avocado, sprouts, and tomato slices. You can always cook up more chicken breasts on the night of to make sure you'll have leftovers.

TOMATO-AVOCADO SALAD

serves 4

This tomato salad topping is about as simple as it gets. More than a recipe, this is a suggestion to toss together whatever raw vegetables you have lying around (especially those that the fruit flies are eyeing up) and pile them on top of sautéed or grilled meat. Don't think twice about adding chopped cucumbers, bell peppers, fresh corn, or herbs to the bowl.

KIDS CAN: Younger helpers can help measure and mix the salad ingredients.

---

2 ripe avocados, pitted and diced

1 pint cherry or grape tomatoes, halved

1 tablespoon olive oil

Big pinch of kosher salt

Freshly ground black pepper

Juice of ½ lime

1 to 2 tablespoons roughly chopped fresh cilantro

---

1. Simply toss everything together just before serving.

SWEET AND SOUR POTATO SALAD

serves 4 to 6

What would summer be without potato salad? Here, warm potatoes are tossed with dill, capers, and tangy dressing. If you're worried that the tart vinaigrette is too much for the little eaters at your table, simply reserve a small bowl of boiled potatoes and drizzle them with olive oil and salt. Using a mix of red and purple potatoes adds a healthy dose of antioxidants to your meal.

- 1½ pounds baby potatoes (any mix of colors)
- 2 teaspoons kosher salt, divided
- ⅓ cup olive oil
- ¼ cup apple cider vinegar
- 1 teaspoon pure cane sugar
- 1 teaspoon Dijon mustard
- ½ cup roughly chopped fresh dill
- ¼ cup drained capers
- 5 to 6 scallions, white and light green parts only, thinly sliced

---

1. Slice the potatoes in half, place them in a large saucepan, and add water to cover by 1 inch. Cover the pot. Bring the water to a boil over high heat, add 1 teaspoon of the salt, then reduce the heat to medium low and simmer, uncovered, until the potatoes are fork-tender—about 7 to 10 minutes. Drain the potatoes and set them aside in a large bowl.

2. While the potatoes are cooking, whisk together the olive oil, vinegar, sugar, mustard, and remaining 1 teaspoon of salt. Stir in the dill, capers, and scallions. Pour the dressing over the warm potatoes, taste, and add more salt if needed. Let the potato salad sit for at least 10 minutes to absorb the dressing, then serve it warm or at room temperature.

The Hays' Family Meal, Wellfleet, Massachusetts

RATATOUILLE PIE

MINT CHOCOLATE CHUNK ICE CREAM

shared by Elspeth Hay

When my youngest daughter, Nora, started daycare, my husband, Alex, and I attended an orientation meeting. One of the questions was about religion. I think the teachers expected us to say something along the lines of "We're atheist," or "Congregationalist," or maybe "lapsed Episcopalian." But instead, my husband turned, looked at me, and said, "Food." Good food is the ethos in our house. My oldest daughter, Sally, has learned to get excited about the seasons, and she knows that late summer is the time for putting things up. She also knows that after all the picking and processing, there's always a big meal to look forward to. In this case, it's a hot, veggie-laden pie with fresh-from-the-garden ice cream for dessert.

RATATOUILLE PIE

makes one 9-inch pie

When I asked my mom for this recipe, she first told me she didn't have one. She did eventually dig it up, but the point is, it's very open to substitutions and variations. If you don't like bacon, it's perfectly good without it, although as a bacon fan I have to say it adds a nice hit of flavor. The bacon can be crumbled into the filling or left as strips and draped across the top.

KIDS CAN: Little ones can crumble the bacon for the bottom of the pie pan.

- 7 slices bacon, cooked and crumbled
- 2 cups Ratatouille Preserves (recipe follows)
- ¼ cup shredded cheese (cheddar or mozzarella both work well)
- 1 pie crust, partially baked (I do this by filling it with weights and baking it for 15 minutes in a 350°F oven)
- 4 large eggs
- 1 to 2 tablespoons whole milk
- 1 to 2 tablespoons unbleached all-purpose flour

---

1. Preheat the oven to 375°F.

2. Combine the bacon, ratatouille preserves, and cheese in a medium bowl and spread this mixture over the bottom of the pie crust.

3. Whisk the eggs, milk, and flour together in a small bowl and pour the egg mixture into the pie crust over the veggies. Bake for 40 minutes, or until the eggs are set and a bit golden on top. Serve warm or chilled.

FOR BABY: Smash bits of pie with the back of a fork or whiz it in a food processor for baby to enjoy.

RATATOUILLE PRESERVES

makes 3 to 4 pints

My mother has been making this recipe for as long as I can remember. She puts it up in pints, as each Ratatouille Pie—essentially a quiche of bacon, cheese, and ratatouille—uses 2 cups of the preserve.

- 1 pound eggplant, cut into ½-inch cubes
- 1 pound zucchini, cut into ½-inch cubes
- 1 tablespoon kosher salt
- 3 tablespoons olive oil, plus more as needed
- 1 pound yellow onions, roughly chopped
- 3 to 4 medium garlic cloves, minced
- 2 pounds tomatoes, cored and roughly chopped
- ¼ pound green or red bell peppers, seeded and roughly chopped (optional)
- Freshly ground black pepper

---

1. In a large colander, toss the eggplant and zucchini with the salt. Let the colander sit in the sink for 15 to 30 minutes, so that the salt can draw the moisture out of the vegetables and the juices can drain. After they have had time to drain, transfer the eggplant and zucchini to a clean dish towel and pat them dry.
2. Place a large, heavy-bottomed pot over medium-high heat, add the olive oil, and drop in the eggplant and zucchini. Sauté for 3 to 4 minutes, until the zucchini is soft and the eggplant is browned. Spoon the vegetables onto a plate and set them aside.
3. Leave the pot over medium-high heat and add in another glug of olive oil. Sauté the onions for 5 to 8 minutes, turning the heat down to medium after a few minutes and sweating them until they get soft and translucent. Add the garlic, sauté for 30 seconds or so, and then add the tomatoes and bell peppers, if using. Cover the pan and cook for 3 to 4 minutes, then take off the lid and turn the heat back up to medium high. Cook, stirring constantly, until the juices have evaporated, about 5 minutes. Add the eggplant and zucchini, then season with salt and pepper to taste. Simmer for another 5 minutes, or until any extra juice evaporates, then turn off the heat and let the mixture cool to room temperature.
4. Pack the ratatouille into pint containers and freeze for up to 8 months or keep refrigerated for 3 to 4 days.

MINT CHOCOLATE CHUNK ICE CREAM

makes about 1 pint

I have long been addicted to Green & Black's Organic Dark Chocolate Mint Bars. I have a square almost every day after lunch. But this recipe might be their true calling. Chopped into bits, some fine and some large, this minty chocolate complements the smooth, sweet cream perfectly and brings out the flavor of the fresh mint. Note that this recipe requires hardly any hands-on time, but it's best to start in the morning or after lunch so that the mint can steep and the ice cream has time to chill before dinner rolls around.

---

2 cups heavy cream
1 cup whole milk
½ cup pure maple syrup
2 cups packed fresh mint leaves
4 ounces mint-flavored dark chocolate, chopped

---

1. Pour the cream, milk, and maple syrup into a medium saucepan. Add the mint leaves, stir, and warm slowly over low heat until the mixture begins to steam. Immediately remove the pan from the heat, cover, and steep for at least 1 hour at room temperature, then transfer the pot to the fridge. When the cream is completely chilled, after about 2 to 3 hours, strain out the mint leaves, wringing them carefully over the pot to release any extra flavor and cream.
2. Pour the strained cream mixture into an ice cream maker and freeze according to the manufacturer's instructions. When the ice cream is almost done, stir in the chocolate.
3. Scoop the ice cream into a container and chill for another hour or so before serving.

A Surprising Meal

ORANGE-GLAZED GRILLED TOFU OVER SUMMER FARRO SALAD

BLENDER CHOCOLATE MOUSSE WITH RASPBERRIES

In July and August, my parents host extended family members, bandmates, and lifelong friends at their house. Come 5:30 P.M., someone starts the grill to prepare a simple, vegetable-focused group dinner. I know the grill is thought of as the mighty meat cooker, but I encourage you to think of it as a big outdoor stove that can transform almost anything (in this case tofu and zucchini) into a summer dinner. For dessert, another surprise: Blender Chocolate Mousse with Raspberries. (Can you guess the secret ingredient?)

ORANGE-GLAZED GRILLED TOFU OVER SUMMER FARRO SALAD

serves 4

Before you turn your nose up at tofu, I want to promise that firm, grilled tofu, drizzled with a soy saucey-gingery-orangey sauce is far from the dreaded world of mushy and bland. In fact, this dish reminds me of the classic Chinese orange chicken that we are all guilty of once ordering at the mall.

KIDS CAN: Bigger kids can shell the pistachio nuts and measure out ¼ cup. Using child-safe knives, kids can slice the zucchini into rounds and then tear up the mint leaves.

---

1 cup farro

1 medium zucchini, cut into ¼-inch-thick rounds

5 tablespoons olive oil, divided

1 block extra-firm tofu, sliced ½ inch thick, then cut in half diagonally

1 cup freshly squeezed orange juice (from about 3 to 4 large oranges)

1-inch piece fresh gingerroot, peeled and grated

2 teaspoons soy sauce

1½ tablespoons rice vinegar

2 teaspoons pure maple syrup

½ teaspoon ground coriander

2 tablespoons minced fresh chives

¼ cup roasted, salted pistachios, chopped

Zest of 1 lemon

¾ teaspoon kosher salt

¼ cup finely chopped fresh mint leaves

---

1. Heat the grill to medium high.
2. While the grill heats up, bring 4 cups of water to a boil in a medium saucepan. Add the farro and cook until tender, about 15 minutes, then drain and set aside at room temperature.
3. In a large bowl, toss the zucchini rounds with 1 tablespoon of olive oil. Brush the tofu triangles with 1 tablespoon of olive oil. Grill the zucchini rounds and tofu triangles in a single layer until grill marks appear, about 5 minutes; flip and repeat on the other side.
4. While the zucchini and tofu cook, whisk together the orange juice, ginger, soy sauce, vinegar, maple syrup, and coriander in a small saucepan. Set the pan over medium-high heat and simmer for 10 minutes, until slightly thickened.
5. Transfer the cooked farro to a serving platter and toss in the grilled zucchini, chives, pistachios, lemon zest, salt, mint leaves, and the remaining 3 tablespoons of olive oil. Arrange the grilled tofu triangles on the salad and spoon the orange sauce over the top. Garnish with some extra pistachios, mint, or chives, if you like.

FOR BABY: Reserve a piece of plain grilled tofu, a few grilled zucchini rounds, and a small bowl of undressed farro. These foods can be pureed, mashed, or cut into bite-size pieces, depending on your baby's age.

BLENDER CHOCOLATE MOUSSE WITH RASPBERRIES

serves 6

This dessert is a magic recipe: you toss a few ingredients into a blender (secret ingredient revealed—avocado!), and in two minutes you have a thick and creamy chocolate mousse sweetened naturally with maple syrup and packed with monounsaturated (healthy) fat. I love to whiz this up after putting the boys to bed, or whenever I'm in need of a guilt-free indulgence. A little taste of the rich mousse goes a long way.

---

1 cup fresh raspberries
3 avocados, peeled and pitted
¼ cup unsweetened cocoa powder
⅔ cup pure maple syrup, plus more for serving
1 teaspoon pure vanilla extract

---

1. In a medium bowl, mash up the raspberries using the back of a fork. You want the berries to break down and release their juices.
2. Whiz the avocados, cocoa, maple syrup, and vanilla in a blender or food processor until smooth.
3. To serve, alternate layers of the chocolate mousse and the mashed raspberries in small bowls and drizzle with extra maple syrup. This treat is best eaten the day it is made.

Summer Party Menu

CLASSIC CAROLINA PULLED PORK SANDWICHES

SIMPLE COLESLAW

QUICK PICKLED CUCUMBERS

FROZEN PEACHES 'N' CREAM CAKE

Dylan's birthday falls at the end of July, and now that he's older he orchestrates his own party. This year was a "Viking-dragon" theme and all he cared about was the cake (chocolate!), but of course we had to feed the crowd as well. This meal hit the party table, and at the end of the evening, there wasn't a bite left. Lucky for me, the main event is a super-simple slow cooker recipe, so all I had to do was toss the coleslaw together and pull out some buns. I used the hours I saved to help paint and hang life-size dragons along our back fence—I don't get to say that every day. Don't forget about the Frozen Peaches 'n' Cream Cake for dessert (you can make it the day before)—it's one of my all-time favorite party sweets. If you are expecting a crowd for anything from a birthday party to a Fourth of July bash, this meal is a natural fit.

CLASSIC CAROLINA PULLED PORK SANDWICHES

serves 10 to 15

The barbecue that is cooked and eaten in the Carolinas is usually pork and typically includes some sort of a spice-and-vinegar liquid. I am partial to this tangy, simple style, which can be easily created in your slow cooker at home using just a few pantry ingredients

1 cup apple cider vinegar
1 tablespoon kosher salt
2 tablespoons brown sugar
One 4- to 5-pound boneless pork butt or shoulder
10 to 15 seeded buns, to serve
Simple Coleslaw (recipe follows)

1. In the bottom of a 6-quart slow cooker insert, whisk together the vinegar, salt, and brown sugar. Add pork and cook on low for 12 hours, until the pork falls apart when pulled with a fork.
2. When the meat is done cooking, transfer it to a large bowl and shred it using 2 forks. Measure out 2 cups of the cooking liquid and discard the rest. Return the reserved 2 cups of liquid and the shredded pork to the slow cooker and stir to combine. Keep the slow cooker on the warm setting until you're ready to eat.
3. To assemble the pulled pork sandwiches, toast the rolls and layer on the pork and coleslaw.

FOR BABY: Babies can enjoy a plate of finely chopped pork and a serving of undressed shredded cabbage and carrots (the tangy coleslaw dressing may be overwhelming). To soften the vegetables, cook a bit of the raw cabbage and carrot mixture in a hot pan with olive oil.

TOMORROW'S DINNER: CARNITAS TACOS

Warm a large cast iron skillet over medium-high heat and toss in the leftover pulled pork. Cook until the edges are crisp. Serve the crispy pork on warm corn tortillas with sliced avocado, cilantro, finely diced onion, and hot sauce.

SIMPLE COLESLAW

tops 10 to 15 sandwiches

Bad coleslaw is a huge turnoff—the globs of mayo and sad, wilted vegetables are just depressing (not to mention unappetizing). This recipe is my attempt at a bright, flavorful, tangy slaw packed with crisp, identifiable vegetables. Naturally, you can pile the slaw onto pork sandwiches, but it is also good on fish tacos or alongside Crispy Seed and Nut-Crusted Chicken (page 168).

- 1 head green cabbage, quartered and cored
- 2 carrots, peeled
- 1 Vidalia onion, peeled and quartered
- ⅓ cup plain full-fat Greek yogurt
- ⅓ cup pure cane sugar
- ⅓ cup Dijon mustard
- ⅓ cup apple cider vinegar
- Kosher salt and freshly ground black pepper

---

1. Shred the cabbage, carrots, and onion using the grating blade attachment on a food processor.
2. In a large bowl, whisk together the yogurt, sugar, mustard, and vinegar. Ten minutes before eating, add the shredded vegetables to the bowl with the dressing and toss well. Taste and season with salt and pepper. The coleslaw is best eaten within 2 hours of assembling.

QUICK PICKLED CUCUMBERS

makes 2 cups

If you like a slightly sweet, fresh pickle, then these will be right up your alley. The ease of this ten-minute recipe always surprises me.

KIDS CAN: Slicing the cucumbers for pickling and placing them into the pickle bath is a good task for kids. Encourage them to taste the raw cucumber and the quick pickle result side-by-side.

½ cup rice wine vinegar
½ cup water
⅓ cup sugar
1 tablespoon kosher salt
2 cups thinly sliced cucumbers
1 thinly sliced red onion or 1 small handful of cilantro (optional)

---

1. Combine the vinegar, water, sugar, and salt in a medium saucepan and bring the mixture to a boil over high heat. Remove the pan from the heat, add the cucumber slices and onion or cilantro, if using, and stir. Cover with a kitchen towel and let the pan rest for 10 minutes before eating. To store extra pickles, pack them into a glass jar with a lid and pour in enough of the pickling liquid to cover them; screw on the lid and refrigerate for up to 1 month.

FOR BABY: Older infants may enjoy a few sticks of raw cucumber to gnaw on.

FROZEN PEACHES 'N' CREAM CAKE

makes one 9-inch cake

This is my favorite make-ahead summer dessert. A simple gingersnap crust is baked in 10 minutes and then filled with rich, creamy, vanilla-spiked peach yogurt. Pop the cake in the freezer, and when you are ready for dessert, the dessert is ready for you. This recipe also makes delicious ice pops. If you want to give the pop version a try, simply drop some gingersnap crumbles into the bottom of the pop molds, pour in the peachy yogurt mixture, insert sticks, and freeze.

KIDS CAN: Small hands can press the crumbled cookie crust into the pan and arrange peach slices on top of the filling.

CRUST

6 tablespoons unsalted butter, melted, plus more for buttering the pan

Two 5.25-ounce packages gingersnap cookies (I like Anna's brand)

FILLING

1 cup heavy cream

2 cups full-fat vanilla yogurt

1 teaspoon pure vanilla extract

2 cups peeled and chopped peaches (about 4 peaches)

1 to 2 peaches, peeled and thinly sliced, for garnish (optional)

1. Preheat the oven to 350°F. Lightly butter a 9-inch springform pan and set it aside.
2. Place the gingersnaps in a food processor and pulse until the cookies resemble coarse sand. Pour in the melted butter and pulse a few times to combine. Transfer the cookie crumbles to the prepared springform pan and, using your fingers, press the crust evenly across the bottom and up the sides. Bake for 10 minutes, then remove the pan from the oven and set it on the counter to cool completely.
3. While the crust bakes, whip the heavy cream in the bowl of an electric mixer until stiff peaks form. In a separate mixing bowl, stir together the yogurt and vanilla extract. Gently fold in the whipped cream, then the chopped peaches.
4. To assemble the cake, pour the filling into the cooled crust. If desired, decorate the top of the pie with additional peach slices. Freeze the cake for at least 4 hours before serving. About 20 minutes before you plan to serve the cake, take it out of the freezer and set it on the counter to soften up (the cake might take more or less time to soften depending on the weather). The softer the cake gets, the more delicious and less icy it is.

FOR BABY: Older infants can try small bites of Peaches 'n' Cream Cake.

Clean Out the Garden Dinner

ZUCCHINI, BEEF, AND HALLOUMI CHEESE SKEWERS WITH CHIMICHURRI SAUCE

TOMATO, PEACH, AND RED ONION PANZANELLA

LEMON-BLACKBERRY CUSTARD

This is a meal I make when we are having friends or family over for a special, grilled dinner in the backyard. Although not complicated, creating the zucchini ribbons, marinating the beef, and chopping the salad ingredients does take a bit of time, so save this meal for a slow afternoon or for when you have some help in the kitchen. Rather than looking at the meal as a series of rigid recipes, I see it as suggestions to (a) grill some halloumi cheese, (b) slather chimichurri sauce on everything, (c) make more panzanella salad, and (d) force everyone to try this custard recipe. Look to your garden (or to your farmers' market or a friend's garden) for any ripe items to string on the skewers, toss into the panzanella, or top the custard. After all, summer is about eating what is ripe that day.

ZUCCHINI, BEEF, AND HALLOUMI CHEESE SKEWERS WITH CHIMICHURRI SAUCE

serves 4

These grilled skewers are completely adaptable—just string on your family's favorites, from cherry tomatoes to cubed chicken thighs. Halloumi cheese, a Greek, semihard cheese, has a high melting point that makes it ideal for grilling. I like to pair the cheese and zucchini with local beef for a dose of vitamin E, beta-carotene, vitamin C, and health-promoting fats. Before marinating all the skewers in chimichurri sauce, taste the sauce to see if it is too strong for your young eaters.

CHIMICHURRI SAUCE

½ cup red wine vinegar

1 teaspoon kosher salt, plus more as needed

3 to 4 garlic cloves, thinly sliced or minced

1 shallot, finely chopped

½ cup minced fresh cilantro

¼ cup minced fresh chives

2 tablespoons finely chopped fresh mint

¾ cup extra virgin olive oil

SKEWERS

1 zucchini

1½ to 2 pounds steak tips

8 ounces halloumi cheese

4 wooden skewers, soaked in water for at least 10 minutes

---

1. Heat the grill to medium high.
2. Make the chimichurri sauce by blending all the ingredients together in a blender or food processor until finely minced.
3. Prepare the ingredients for the skewers. First, using a vegetable peeler, peel the zucchini into a pile of thin ribbons. Cut the steak and halloumi cheese into 1-inch cubes.
4. Assemble the 4 skewers, alternating between the zucchini ribbons, beef, and cheese. Pour the chimichurri sauce into a shallow platter, reserving ½ cup in a small bowl. Roll the assembled skewers in the sauce on the platter, cover, and refrigerate for 10 minutes or up to a few hours in the refrigerator.
5. Grill the skewers for 5 minutes per side, brushing them occasionally with the reserved chimichurri sauce, until grill marks appear and the beef is medium rare. Serve hot or warm with reserved chimichurri sauce on the side.

FOR BABY: Grill one skewer without chimichurri sauce for baby (simply brush it with olive oil). Remove the grilled beef, zucchini, and cheese from the skewer and dice it or puree the mixture in a food processor.

TOMORROW'S DINNER: CRAZY CHEF'S SALAD

Tear up a few heads of romaine lettuce and place it in a large bowl. Toss in leftover grilled beef, zucchini, and halloumi cheese. Add some torn bread, olives, nuts or seeds, chopped tomatoes, and cucumber. Dress the salad with lemon juice and olive oil.

TOMATO, PEACH, AND RED ONION PANZANELLA

serves 4 to 6

This summer panzanella salad is packed with tomatoes and peaches—a seemingly strange combination, but one on which you'll soon be hooked. I always think that if two foods are growing and ripe at the same time, they must be a good match.

KIDS CAN: Little ones of all ages can tear French bread for salad.

---

1 French baguette, torn into 1-inch pieces (about 6 cups)

½ cup olive oil, divided

¾ teaspoon kosher salt, divided, plus more as needed

3 large tomatoes or 3 cups cherry tomatoes, sliced

3 large peaches, pitted and sliced

3 tablespoons red wine vinegar

¼ teaspoon freshly ground black pepper, plus more as needed

½ red onion, thinly sliced

½ cup chopped fresh basil

---

1. Preheat the oven to 400°F.

2. In a large bowl, toss the bread pieces with 2 tablespoons of the olive oil, then sprinkle with ¼ teaspoon of salt. Arrange the bread on a rimmed baking sheet in a single layer. Bake for 20 minutes, stirring halfway, or until evenly toasted.

3. In a large bowl, gently toss the tomatoes and peaches with the remaining ½ teaspoon of salt. Transfer the tomato-peach mix to a colander set over another large bowl; set it aside to drain while the bread toasts.

4. Lift the colander of peaches and tomatoes out of the bowl and set it aside. Whisk the remaining 6 tablespoons of oil, the vinegar, and the black pepper into the tomato-peach juices. Add the toasted bread pieces, toss to coat, and let them soak for 10 minutes, tossing occasionally. Add the tomatoes and peaches, red onion, and basil to the bowl with the bread and toss to combine. Season with salt and pepper to taste and serve immediately.

FOR BABY: Set aside a few extra peach slices for finger food.

LEMON-BLACKBERRY CUSTARD

serves 6

This custard knocks it out of the park. The top of the custard is fluffy and set, but when you dig your spoon in you find a tart lemon cream—it's like magic. If your blueberry or raspberry bushes are bursting with fruit, by all means toss those in, too.

KIDS CAN: Older children can make the whipped cream for dessert.

---

3 tablespoons unsalted butter, at room temperature, plus more for greasing the pan

½ cup pure cane sugar

2½ teaspoons freshly grated lemon zest

3 large eggs, separated

3 tablespoons unbleached all-purpose flour

1 cup buttermilk

¼ cup freshly squeezed lemon juice

1 cup fresh blackberries (or any fresh summer berry), plus more for serving

Whipped cream, for serving

---

1. Preheat the oven to 350°F. Grease an 8-inch pie pan with butter.
2. In the bowl of an electric mixer, beat together the sugar, butter, and lemon zest. Beat in the egg yolks, then add one-third of the flour followed by one-half of the buttermilk, beating well after each addition. Continue alternating between the flour and buttermilk, then turn off the mixer and stir in the lemon juice.
3. In a new bowl, using clean beaters and the electric mixer, beat the egg whites until stiff, glossy peaks form. Fold the egg whites into the batter. Pour the custard batter into the buttered pie pan and top with the berries. Place the custard pan in a roasting pan or large skillet (whatever fits). Add enough water to the roasting pan to come halfway up the sides of the pie pan. Bake the custard until it is set in the center and just begins to brown, about 40 minutes. Serve with fresh whipped cream and blackberries.

Low-Stress Dinner for a Stressful Day

SLOW COOKER GREEK CHICKEN GYROS

ROASTED GREEN BEANS WITH SCALLIONS

FROZEN MELON BALLS

This is the dinner for your busiest night of the week. The chicken cooks itself on your counter, and come dinnertime, all you have to do is stir together a quick lemon-yogurt sauce, chop a few summer vegetables for toppings (or better yet—get the kids to chop the vegetables), and throw the green beans in the oven. You can easily pack this meal up to bring to the beach or park, as everything tastes good warm, at room temperature, or chilled. And yes, "stress" is in the title, so naturally wine is included in the dessert.

SLOW COOKER GREEK CHICKEN GYROS

makes about 8 gyros

Every Sunday I ask Nick and the boys to help draft a list of dinners for the week ahead. Nine times out of ten, these chicken gyros are first on Nick's list—so often that is has become a running joke. But he's right: they are really good and incredibly simple to plan for and prepare. A total win across the board.

CHICKEN

2 medium yellow onions, thinly sliced

2 pounds boneless, skinless chicken breasts or thighs, cut into 1-inch pieces

Juice of 2 lemons

1 tablespoon olive oil

1 teaspoon chopped fresh oregano

3 tablespoons chopped fresh dill

1 teaspoon kosher salt

¼ teaspoon freshly ground black pepper

LEMON-YOGURT SAUCE

1 cup plain full-fat Greek yogurt

Juice of 1 lemon

Kosher salt and freshly ground black pepper

TO ASSEMBLE

Lavash or pita bread, warmed (1 per person)

Chopped tomatoes

Chopped cucumber

Minced yellow onion

Pitted Kalamata olives

Baby arugula

Lemon slices, for serving (optional)

---

1. In a 6-quart slow cooker, combine the onions, chicken, lemon juice, olive oil, oregano, dill, salt, and pepper. Cover and cook on low for 4 to 6 hours, until chicken can be easily shredded with a fork. Before serving, taste and add more salt, pepper, fresh dill, or lemon juice as needed.
2. To make the sauce, whisk together the yogurt, lemon juice, salt, and pepper in a medium bowl. Sauce can be made ahead and kept, covered in the fridge, for up to 3 days.
3. To assemble the gyros, spread some of the lemon-yogurt sauce onto each piece of lavash or pita, add a few forkfuls of chicken, and top with chopped tomatoes, cucumber, onion, olives, and baby arugula. Squirt with more lemon juice if you like.

FOR BABY: Finely shred some chicken for baby, tossing in a little yogurt if you'd like. Serve with small bites of cucumber and melon.

TOMORROW'S DINNER: GREEK PIZZA

Top rolled-out pizza dough with leftover chopped chicken, feta cheese, Kalamata olives, and sautéed spinach. Bake and serve with a simple tomato–red onion salad.

ROASTED GREEN BEANS WITH SCALLIONS

serves 4

For those of you who don't typically care for green beans, I challenge you to try this side dish. The green beans and scallions become soft, caramelized, and packed with flavor.

---

1 pound green beans, trimmed

6 scallions, root ends trimmed and all but 1 inch of their dark green tops removed, halved lengthwise

¼ cup olive oil

½ teaspoon kosher salt

Freshly ground black pepper

---

1. Preheat the oven to 375°F.
2. Toss everything together and arrange the mixture in a single layer on a rimmed baking sheet or in a roasting pan. Roast in the oven, tossing every 10 minutes, for 20 to 30 minutes, until vegetables are very soft and caramelized.

FROZEN MELON BALLS

serves 8 to 10

I recently fell in love with the retro melon ball—or, I should say, I fell in love with our boys' interest in scooping melon balls. They will sit with halved melons and the baller tool and go to town, leaving me in peace to get dinner under way. Of course the balls are oddly formed and totally manhandled, but they are delicious frozen on sticks nonetheless. Kids can nibble on the frozen melon balls, while grown-ups pop them into glasses of chilled rosé or white wine.

---

1 watermelon

1 cantaloupe

1 honeydew

---

1. Using a melon baller, scoop balls of watermelon, cantaloupe, and honeydew. Skewer the melon onto short wooden sticks (I like 4-inch skewers that fit 3 balls or 6-inch skewers that fit 5 balls) and lay the sticks on a parchment-lined dish. You can skewer any combination of melon you like. Freeze the melon balls for 1½ to 2 hours.

NOTE: Large melon balls, when frozen, can be a choking hazard for little ones. You can cut the balls up and skewer them in smaller bites or remove the large frozen balls from the skewers, smash them with the back of a fork, and serve them that way.

Grandma's Flounder with Pink Salad

15-MINUTE FLOUNDER

PINK SALAD

This simple fish dinner is inspired by a dish my mother-in-law, Polly, cooks for us every summer in Truro. We sit at her counter, she pops a tray of flounder in the oven, and fifteen minutes later we chow down with the coral sunset behind us. To take advantage of summer melons and berries, I serve Polly's flounder with a raw watermelon and raspberry fruit salad sprinkled with feta cheese, toasted hazelnuts, and fresh mint. Summer meals and moments like this are exactly what I try to imagine, with eyes closed, whenever I find myself surrounded by piles of laundry in my dark living room in the middle of February.

15-MINUTE FLOUNDER

serves 4

The trick to this recipe is layering the thin flounder fillets on top of each other, sandwiched with mustard and panko bread crumbs, and then baking them at a high heat. This simple technique takes the stress out of preparing fish for a crowd (no delicate sautéing of individual fillets) and results in a perfectly cooked, flavorful meal. You can substitute the Dijon mustard for honey mustard, pesto, or a flavored butter, if you'd like.

KIDS CAN: Ask your helpers to brush the fish with mustard and sprinkle on the bread crumbs.

---

2 tablespoons olive oil, divided
8 flounder fillets (2 per person)
4 tablespoons Dijon mustard
Kosher salt and freshly ground black pepper
½ cup panko bread crumbs
1 lemon, sliced into wedges

---

1. Preheat the oven to 425°F and rub 1 tablespoon of olive oil across a rimmed baking sheet.
2. Lay 4 of the fish fillets in a row on the oiled pan. Brush a bit of mustard onto each fillet, then sprinkle the tops with salt and pepper. Place 1 tablespoon of the panko bread crumbs atop each fillet and spread the bread crumbs out with your fingers. Top each breaded fillet with another flounder fillet and repeat with the remaining mustard, salt, pepper, and bread crumbs. To finish, drizzle the remaining 1 tablespoon of olive oil over the top of the fillets.
3. Bake the fish for 10 to 15 minutes, until the tops are slightly golden and the fish is easily flaked with a fork. During the last minute of baking, turn on the broiler for a crisp top.

FOR BABY: Cut a small piece of flounder, brush it with olive oil, and cook it alongside the others. Flake the fish into tiny pieces for baby's dinner. Serve with diced or mashed watermelon and raspberries.

PINK SALAD

serves 4 to 6

I can't help but love a *pink* salad (says the only girl in her household). But really, this is just a tricky way to make a regular old summer fruit salad feel new and exciting.

KIDS CAN: Young helpers can squish and squeeze the lime in a citrus juicer.

---

2 cups cubed fresh watermelon

1 cup fresh raspberries

½ cup crumbled feta cheese

½ cup hazelnuts, toasted and roughly chopped

¼ cup finely chopped fresh mint leaves

Juice of 1 lime

3 tablespoons olive oil

Kosher salt and freshly ground black pepper

---

1. Gently toss everything together and serve immediately.

Summer Sunday Supper

HOMEMADE PASTA WITH HEIRLOOM TOMATO SAUCE

PAVLOVA WITH BLUEBERRY SAUCE

I am the home cook in our house, preparing the daily meals, from quick smoothies before school to packed lunch boxes and nightly dinners. Nick does not cook for our family on a daily basis, but he does take on monumental cooking projects, producing some of the best meals I've ever had. He takes over the kitchen on Sunday afternoons to experiment with his latest food obsession. Lucky for us, making homemade pasta has occupied his free time for a few years now. Our kids love helping to mix, roll, and cut the sheets of pasta, and, for me, seeing our boys spend an afternoon with Daddy in the kitchen is about as good as it gets (and that's not just my full belly of fettuccine talking).

HOMEMADE PASTA WITH HEIRLOOM TOMATO SAUCE

serves 4 to 6

This is Nick's favorite pasta recipe and technique. Of course, you can serve this pasta with anything you like—from basil pesto to meat sauce or just good olive oil and Parmesan cheese—but in August, when tomatoes are ripe, this raw, fresh-from-the-garden sauce is what we crave.

KIDS CAN: Young cooks can measure ingredients and roll out and cut the pasta.

PASTA

4 cups unbleached all-purpose flour

4 large eggs

Semolina flour, for dusting

SAUCE

3 large vine-ripened tomatoes

1 teaspoon kosher salt

½ teaspoon freshly ground black pepper

1 large garlic clove

Juice of ½ lemon

3 tablespoons olive oil

1 small bunch basil

Freshly grated Parmesan cheese, for serving

---

1. This whole process can be done directly on a work surface, but it takes some practice. I like to make the pasta in a bowl to keep everything contained. First, put flour in a large, shallow mixing bowl. Create a well with 2 fingers in the center of the flour for the eggs.
2. Crack the eggs into the well. With a fork, break the yolks and begin to mix the eggs, slowly incorporating flour from the sides. Continue to mix until about half of the flour is incorporated. At this point you can dump the mixture out onto a work surface or leave it in the bowl. Either way, continue to work the flour and eggs together into a ball.
3. When a rough ball has formed, set it aside and scrape off and discard the excess flour on your work surface or in your bowl. Knead the ball with the palm of your hand for 10 minutes, until the dough is smooth and has some elasticity. Wrap the dough in plastic wrap and set it aside at room temperature for at least 30 minutes. Dough can rest up to 60 minutes at room temperature or up to 1 day in the fridge (let it stand at room temperature for 1 hour before rolling).
4. Meanwhile, make the sauce. Cut the tomatoes into medium-size dice and place them in a large bowl. Add the salt and pepper and mix well. The salt will help the tomatoes release their water, which turns into the sauce.
5. Using a microplane, grate the garlic directly into the bowl with the tomatoes. (Since the sauce isn't cooked, it's nice to use the microplane

to avoid biting into bits of raw garlic.) Squeeze in the lemon juice and add a good amount of olive oil. Mix thoroughly and let the sauce marinate while you roll out the pasta.

6. Prepare your pasta machine on the widest setting. Cut the ball of dough into 4 equal pieces. You'll work with only 1 ball at a time; keep the other 3 wrapped so they don't dry out.

7. Lightly flour the dough ball and, using the palm of your hand, press it out into a rough, ⅛-inch-thick rectangle. Run the dough through the widest setting of the machine. Fold the dough into thirds and repeat 3 to 4 times, changing the orientation each time. Run the pasta sheets once through each subsequent setting, making the pasta dough thinner and thinner, dusting it lightly with flour as necessary. Our pasta maker has 9 settings, and we like the thinnest for fettucine. By the time you get to the last setting, the dough will be very long. Divide it into 8-inch pieces before cutting it into fettuccine.

8. Attach the fettuccine attachment to your pasta machine and cut each 8-inch piece of dough. Dust the fettuccine with semolina flour, bunch them into little nests, and let them rest on a semolina-dusted baking sheet or tray. Repeat with the remaining balls of dough.

9. Bring a heavily salted pot of water to a boil, add the pasta nests in one at a time, stir, and cook for about 1 minute, until the water comes back up to a boil and the pasta begins to float. Drain.

10. Right before you're ready to eat, cut or tear the basil and add it to the tomato sauce; mix well. Add the pasta to the sauce and mix thoroughly, coating everything. Portion the pasta and sauce into bowls and grate a good amount of Parmesan cheese on top of each serving. Devour.

FOR BABY: Toss a bit of plain pasta with olive oil, then cut or mash it into appropriate bites.

PAVLOVA WITH BLUEBERRY SAUCE

serves 6 to 8

Because this Sunday dinner feels so special to me, I've included a beloved dessert recipe to cap it off: Pavlova with Blueberry Sauce. If I were stranded on a desert island with just one precious sweet, this pavlova would be it. The recipe yields a meringue that is crisp on the outside and soft and spongy in the middle—top that with sweetened whipped cream and blueberry sauce and you have the ultimate summer dessert.

MERINGUE

1 teaspoon pure vanilla extract

1 teaspoon white vinegar

1 cup pure cane sugar

1½ teaspoons arrowroot powder

4 large egg whites

Pinch of kosher salt

BLUEBERRY SAUCE

1 cup fresh blueberries

½ cup water

Squeeze of lemon juice

2 tablespoons Vanilla Sugar (page 107) or pure cane sugar

WHIPPED CREAM

1 cup heavy whipping cream

1 tablespoon pure cane sugar

1 teaspoon pure vanilla extract

---

1. Place a rack in the center of the oven and preheat to 275°F. Line a rimmed baking sheet with parchment paper and draw a 7-inch circle on the paper. Flip the paper so no pen or pencil gets on the food.

2. To make the meringue, mix the vanilla and vinegar in a small cup. In a separate bowl, stir the arrowroot powder into the sugar.

3. Combine the egg whites and salt in the bowl of an electric mixer fitted with the whisk attachment. Whip on medium-low speed until soft peaks form, approximately 2 to 3 minutes. Increase the speed to medium high, and with the motor running, slowly sprinkle in the sugar-arrowroot mixture. Beat for 2 more minutes, then slowly pour in the vanilla and vinegar. Increase the speed to high and whip the mixture until stiff, glossy peaks form when the whisk is lifted, 4 to 5 minutes.

4. Gently spread the meringue inside the circle drawn on the parchment paper, making sure the edges of the meringue are slightly higher than the center. (You want a slight well in the center of the meringue in which to place the whipped cream and fruit.) Bake for 65 minutes. Turn off the heat, leave the door slightly ajar, and let the meringue cool completely in the oven. Wash and dry the mixer bowl and whisk attachment.

5. To make the blueberry sauce, combine all the ingredients in a small saucepan over medium-

high heat. Bring the mixture to a boil, reduce the heat to low, and simmer for 10 minutes, until slightly thickened and fragrant. Remove the pan from the heat and let the blueberry sauce cool completely (you can stick the pan in the freezer to speed it along).

6. To make the whipped cream, pour the heavy cream, sugar, and vanilla into the bowl of an electric mixer fitted with the whisk attachment. Beat the mixture at high speed until soft peaks form.

7. To assemble the pavlova, scoop the whipped cream onto the meringue and top with the cooled blueberry sauce. Serve immediately.

Fall

The start of fall is in many ways the mark of a new year for busy families. School starts, regular family rhythms return, and schedules are packed with afternoon activities. I find myself making more promises and resolutions in the fall than in January: *I will finish cleaning the basement* and *We will have fish for dinner once a week* are perennial favorites. Fall gives us the chance to start fresh—set new goals, revise family strategies, and kick off invigorating resolutions. It is a great time to dive into household and cooking projects that will make the adjustment to school life easier—get rid of all those packable containers you don't use and make a pot of rice and beans every Sunday, for a start. Happily, the season graciously rewards our busy lives with magnificent produce. Apples, cranberries, squash, pears, and pumpkins are ready to harvest and enjoy in lunchboxes and at dinnertime. It is the perfect opportunity to tighten up your meal planning and organization to insure that you don't lose your sanity. After a summer full of raw and cool foods, fall dinners, such as Lentil and Chard Soup with Pumpkin Seed–Cheddar Crisps (page 235) and Beet and Potato Hash with Eggs (page 248), are even more welcoming. And desserts? As far as I'm concerned, fall should be renamed "the season of baked orchard fruit." Whether you are looking for a fresh Thanksgiving dessert, planning ahead for the holiday season, or just want your house to smell really, really great, simple sweets like Cranberry-Apple Crumble with Gingersnaps (page 237) require little hands-on time but are full of the quintessential fall flavors.

Fall Meals

Fritters and Chocolate (Need I Say More?)

BROCCOLI AND CAULIFLOWER FRITTERS

PANTRY CLEAN-OUT CHOCOLATE BARK

Oftentimes the back-to-school routine takes me by surprise. By the end of the summer I am ready for a sense of routine, but then it hits and I am shaken up by the fact that life is *really* busy. Our home cooking often suffers during these first few weeks, as we get our school feet back under us. This year, I woke up one September morning *determined* to get some home-cooked green vegetables into the boys that day and knew fritters were the way to do it. We made these fritters, sliced up a big bowl of orchard fruit (pears, apples, and late peaches), and chowed down. Afterward, we celebrated surviving another Wednesday with a tray of Pantry Clean-Out Chocolate Bark.

BROCCOLI AND CAULIFLOWER FRITTERS

makes 8 small fritters

I vividly remember the day I finalized this fritter recipe. I made a batch while Dylan was at school and Gray was asleep upstairs. Eight fritters, warm and crispy, lay in front of me. I ate six of them, one after the other, still standing at the stove in the midst of a dirty kitchen. An hour later, Gray woke up and happily chowed down fritter number seven. I hid number eight in the back of the fridge because I desperately wanted Nick to try one but knew if it was within our sight it would be gone by 6 P.M. when he got home. Happily, the last fritter survived the afternoon, so Nick could give the recipe his blessing. Now, whenever I plan on Broccoli and Cauliflower Fritters for dinner, I wait until everyone is home before I pan-fry the patties—it's only fair.

KIDS CAN: Little helpers can smash the fritter mixture with a potato masher.

1½ cups bite-size broccoli florets

1½ cups bite-size cauliflower florets

1 large egg

½ cup unbleached all-purpose flour

⅓ cup finely grated Parmesan cheese

1 small garlic clove, minced

½ teaspoon kosher salt, plus more as needed

Several grinds of black pepper

3 to 4 tablespoons canola oil, for frying

LEMON-YOGURT SAUCE

Juice of 1 lemon

1 cup plain full-fat Greek yogurt or sour cream

---

1. To make the fritters, bring ½ inch of water to a boil in a large saucepan. Add the broccoli and cauliflower, cover the pan, and boil the vegetables for 5 minutes. Remove the pan from the heat and drain the vegetables, then pat them dry with clean kitchen towels.
2. While the vegetables cook, beat the egg lightly in a large mixing bowl. Add in the flour, cheese, garlic, salt, pepper, and cooked broccoli and cauliflower. Using a potato masher, mash everything together. You want the broccoli and cauliflower to be recognizable but broken down.
3. Heat 3 tablespoons of canola oil in a large, heavy skillet over medium heat. Once the oil is hot, scoop out a mound of the batter (about 2 tablespoons) and drop it into the pan, then flatten it slightly with your spoon or spatula. Repeat with more of the batter, spacing the fritters 2 inches apart on all sides. Once the fritters have browned underneath, after about 2 minutes, flip them and cook on the other side until

golden, another 2 minutes. Repeat with the remaining batter, adding more oil if needed.

4. To make the sauce, whisk together the lemon juice and yogurt in a small bowl.

5. Serve the hot fritters with the sauce for dipping.

FOR BABY: Smash a fritter with the back of a fork to make little bits for baby. Older infants may like to hold a whole fritter and feed themselves.

PANTRY CLEAN-OUT CHOCOLATE BARK

makes one 9 by 12-inch slab of bark

You know when pantry jars are left with just a couple of tablespoons of nuts, seeds, or dried fruit? Oh, the prized shelf space gone to ruin! My solution is to toss all those little bits onto melted chocolate and make a tray of bark. Here, I mention four of my favorite combinations, but I'm willing to bet anything stored in your pantry tastes even better sprinkled on semisweet chocolate.

KIDS CAN: As there is no wrong way to sprinkle fruit and nuts onto chocolate, little kitchen helpers are especially good at taking on this project and making a custom piece of edible art. This recipe has rescued me and the boys from many grumpy afternoons.

---

1 pound semisweet chocolate

SUGGESTED TOPPINGS

1 tablespoon granola

1 tablespoon pistachios + 1 tablespoon dried cherries

1 tablespoon roasted and salted pepitas + 1 tablespoon dried cranberries

1 tablespoon roasted and salted peanuts + 1 tablespoon unsweetened shredded coconut

---

1. Line a rimmed baking sheet with parchment paper, letting it hang over the long sides.
2. Roughly chop the chocolate. Bring a small pot of water to a boil and place a metal bowl over the pot. Put the chopped chocolate in the bowl and stir it over the heat until it is completely melted. Pour the melted chocolate onto the parchment paper–lined tray and spread it evenly with a spatula. You are aiming for a ⅛-inch-thick rectangle.
3. Sprinkle your chosen toppings over the chocolate, then refrigerate for at least 1 hour or until firm. When you're ready to eat, lift the bark out of the pan by grabbing the long ends of the parchment paper and break the bark into shards. Extra bark can be stored in an airtight container on the counter for up to 1 week.

FOR BABY: Offer baby a sampling of appropriate chocolate bark toppings, such as dried fruit and seeds.

Not-Boring Steak and Potatoes

GRANDMA'S SKIRT STEAK

LEMON-TAHINI SWEET POTATOES AND CHICKPEAS

In our early twenties, Nick and I bounced around between apartments, jobs, and graduate schools. We were short on time and money but deeply in love with cooking, and we made dinner together every night. This meal is one that we made back then and still do today. The ingredients are simple and easy to find, and the meal feels fancy (steak has a way of doing that), even though it's really just a basic, thirty-minute dinner. Grandma's Skirt Steak recipe is borrowed from my mother-in-law, and the sweet potato-chickpea side is inspired by a warm salad my sister first made for us. Both recipes are oldies but goodies and are still family favorites after a decade.

GRANDMA'S SKIRT STEAK

serves 4

Skirt steak is a lean, thin, long cut of beef with an intense beefy flavor. It is a tough muscle, so the steak should be cooked to rare or medium-rare doneness and then cut against the grain for a tender bite. As skirt steak takes well to marinades, you can adapt this simple one by adding in sesame oil, scallions, garlic, freshly squeezed orange juice, or red pepper flakes.

---

1 pound local skirt steak
Juice of 1 lime
¼ cup low-sodium soy sauce

---

1. Using a sharp knife, poke a series of small holes on both sides of the steak. In a shallow baking dish, whisk together the lime juice and soy sauce. Lay the steak in the marinade and let it sit out at room temperature for 15 minutes (flipping it halfway) while you prepare the sweet potatoes. If you marinate the steak any longer than 15 minutes, it will be too salty.

2. After the steak is done marinating, heat an oiled grill pan over medium-high heat. Grill the skirt steak for 3 minutes per side. (This cooking time results in a medium-rare steak. Add a minute to each side for a medium steak.) Transfer the steak to a cutting board and let it sit for 5 to 10 minutes, then slice it thinly against the grain.

TOMORROW'S DINNER: STEAK FAJITAS

Thinly slice bell peppers and onions and caramelize them in a hot skillet. Serve the soft vegetables with leftover steak and warm flour tortillas.

LEMON-TAHINI SWEET POTATOES AND CHICKPEAS

serves 4

This recipe is extremely adaptable. The idea here is to pair a root vegetable or squash with a legume, and toss those goodies together with fresh herbs and a nutty, creamy tahini dressing. If there are parts of this warm salad that little ones would prefer served plain, simply reserve a small portion of roasted sweet potatoes or chickpeas before mixing the salad together.

KIDS CAN: Kids can peel the sweet potatoes, chop the cilantro with child-safe knives, and whisk together the sauce.

- 2 sweet potatoes, peeled and cut into ½-inch cubes
- 2 tablespoons olive oil
- Pinch of kosher salt
- One 15-ounce can chickpeas, drained and rinsed
- 1 shallot, minced
- 3 tablespoons roughly chopped fresh cilantro

DRESSING

- 1 garlic clove, minced or grated on a microplane
- Zest and juice of 1 lemon
- 3 tablespoons tahini
- 2 tablespoons warm water
- 2 tablespoons olive oil
- ¼ teaspoon kosher salt

---

1. Preheat the oven to 425°F. On a large rimmed baking sheet, toss the sweet potato cubes with the olive oil and salt. Arrange the potatoes in a single layer and roast until golden and tender, about 20 minutes. Remove the potatoes from the oven and transfer them to a large serving bowl.
2. To make the dressing, combine all the ingredients in a lidded glass jar, screw on the top, and shake well.
3. Add the chickpeas, shallot, and cilantro to the bowl with the potatoes. Drizzle the tahini dressing over top and serve immediately.

FOR BABY: Reserve a handful of roasted sweet potato cubes and drained chickpeas for baby. You can toss the potatoes and chickpeas with olive oil if you'd like.

For That Perfect Fall Day

LENTIL AND CHARD SOUP

PUMPKIN SEED-CHEDDAR CRISPS

CRANBERRY-APPLE CRUMBLE WITH GINGERSNAPS

Soup is one of those magical things (along with smoothies) that my kids will eat even when packed with unfamiliar vegetables. However, if said vegetables are too big to fit on their little soup spoons, then it's game-over. Through the years, I have learned my lesson: if I want the kids to dig into their bowls, the soup elements have to be small and easily scoopable. I often use a food processor to whiz the veggies before adding them to the pot—to save both time and energy. To make this simple soup dinner a little special, I have included our recipe for Pumpkin Seed-Cheddar Crisps. These thin, salty disks of cheese float on and then melt into the hot soup. If you only have time to prepare for the soup, then try another surprising (no-cook) soup topper like popcorn, leftover crumbled bacon, or lemony sour cream.

LENTIL AND CHARD SOUP

serves 4 to 6

This soup is my solution for using up leftover cooked grains from a previous meal or an ambitious weekend prep session. Here, I call for precooked long-grain rice, but you can use any whole grain you like, from wild rice to farro or barley.

- 3 tablespoons olive oil
- ⅔ cup green lentils
- 1 medium yellow onion, finely chopped
- 1 garlic clove, finely chopped
- 2 celery ribs, finely chopped
- 2 carrots, peeled and finely chopped
- 1 bunch (about 7 stalks) Swiss chard, leaves removed from the stems and sliced into thin ribbons
- 1 teaspoon kosher salt
- Freshly ground black pepper
- 2 tablespoons tomato paste
- Pinch of ground cumin
- 6½ cups low-sodium vegetable broth
- 1 cup cooked rice or grain (see Note)
- Juice of ½ lemon
- Pumpkin Seed–Cheddar Crisps (recipe follows)

NOTE: If you do not have 1 cup of precooked rice hanging around, simply pour ½ cup of long-grain rice and 1 cup of water into a small saucepan. Bring the water to a boil, then reduce the heat to low, cover the pan, and simmer for 30 minutes or until the water is absorbed and the rice is tender.

1. Heat the oil in a large soup pot over medium-high heat. Add in the lentils, onion, garlic, celery, and carrots. Cook, stirring occasionally, for 7 to 10 minutes, until the vegetables are lightly browned. Stir in the Swiss chard, salt, and a few grinds of pepper. Cook for 2 to 3 minutes more, then add the tomato paste, cumin, and broth. Bring the soup to a boil, turn the heat to medium low, and simmer, partially covered, for 20 to 25 minutes, until the vegetables are soft and the broth reduces slightly. Stir in the rice and lemon juice and cook for a few more minutes or until everything is heated through.
2. Taste and adjust the seasonings as necessary, then ladle the soup into bowls and top with Pumpkin Seed–Cheddar Crisps.

FOR BABY: Older infants can feed themselves a bowl of soup, while younger babies will benefit from a smoother serving that has been whizzed in the food processor or blender.

PUMPKIN SEED–CHEDDAR CRISPS

makes 8 crisps

This recipe is a simple mix of four ingredients and calls for some good, old-fashioned dumping and piling, making it a perfect kitchen project for young helpers.

KIDS CAN: Children can take on this whole recipe—measuring ingredients, making mounds on the baking sheet, and flattening the crisps before baking.

- ¼ cup pepitas (hulled pumpkin seeds)
- ½ cup shredded sharp cheddar cheese
- ½ cup freshly grated Romano cheese
- ¼ cup panko bread crumbs

---

1. Preheat the oven to 325°F. Line a rimmed baking sheet with parchment paper.
2. In a small bowl, mix together the pepitas, cheddar and Romano cheeses, and bread crumbs. Scoop the mixture into 8 equal-size piles on the baking sheet and slightly flatten the mounds with the back of a measuring cup.
3. Bake for 15 minutes, until the cheese has melted and the edges are golden and crispy. Remove the crisps from the oven and let them cool slightly on the tray before using. Extra crisps can be stored in an airtight container at room temperature for up to 3 days.

CRANBERRY-APPLE CRUMBLE WITH GINGERSNAPS

serves 6

I get that you may not have time for a crumble dessert on an average weeknight, but this is the time to dream those holiday baking dreams. Maybe a few test bakes on dark afternoons isn't so bad? Really, the time investment here lies in peeling the apples, so make sure to rope in any available helpers.

KIDS CAN: Little ones can peel the apples and crush the gingersnap cookies.

CRUMBLE TOPPING

½ cup unbleached all-purpose flour

¼ cup coconut sugar

3 tablespoons packed brown sugar

1 cup gingersnap crumbs (from 4 ounces of cookies; I like Anna's Ginger Thins)

¼ cup pecans, roughly chopped (optional)

⅛ teaspoon ground ginger

⅛ teaspoon kosher salt

½ cup (1 stick) cold unsalted butter, cut into ½-inch cubes

FILLING

6 medium apples (I like Honeycrisp or Pink Lady), peeled, cored, and cut into ¼-inch-thick slices (about 4 cups sliced)

1½ cups fresh cranberries

Zest and juice of ½ lemon

½ teaspoon pure vanilla extract

¼ cup coconut sugar

¼ cup packed brown sugar

2 tablespoons arrowroot powder

Whipped cream or vanilla ice cream, for serving (optional)

---

1. Preheat the oven to 350°F.

2. To make the crumble topping, stir together the flour, coconut sugar, brown sugar, gingersnap crumbs, pecans (if using), ginger, and salt in a large bowl. Toss in the butter cubes and mix to distribute evenly.

3. In an 8 by 11-inch baking dish, mix together the sliced apples, cranberries, lemon zest and juice, vanilla, sugars, and arrowroot powder, then spread the mixture evenly in the pan.

4. Sprinkle the crumble topping over the fruit. Bake for 45 minutes, until you see juices bubbling through the topping. Remove the crumble from the oven and let it cool slightly, then serve it warm with whipped cream or vanilla ice cream.

FOR BABY: Dig out a few sweet, soft apple slices from the bottom of the crisp for a special dessert.

FRESH
LOCAL
SEAFOOD

The Kenners' Family Meal, Providence, Rhode Island

FISH CHOWDER WITH CORN AND SAFFRON

APPLE LOAF CAKE

shared by Ashley Kenner

We feel very lucky that our house is just a few blocks from the city's largest outdoor farmers' market. We make a Saturday family routine out of walking through the stalls, getting breakfast sandwiches and frozen lemonade, and stocking up on fresh goodies for the week. I created this soup dinner as a way to showcase the fresh fish we are surrounded by in Rhode Island. It doesn't hurt that I come from a family of soup lovers (we celebrate each year with a holiday/high-stakes competition called Soup Day), so I am naturally drawn to this simple, one-pot meal.

FISH CHOWDER WITH CORN AND SAFFRON

serves 6

This fish chowder is inspired by a chicken soup I used to make when I worked as a nanny. The saffron and corn complement the fish even more beautifully than they did the chicken in my original recipe, and the whole thing comes together in just about fifteen minutes, making it the perfect quick family dinner.

- 2 tablespoons unsalted butter or extra virgin olive oil
- 1 medium onion, diced
- 2 celery ribs, diced
- 1 tablespoon fresh thyme leaves
- 1 tablespoon unbleached all-purpose flour
- 1 quart seafood stock (homemade or store-bought)
- Pinch of saffron threads
- 2 to 3 fillets of haddock, cod, flounder, sole, or whatever firm white fish you prefer, cut into 2-inch chunks
- 2 cups corn kernels (fresh is best but frozen is also fine)
- ½ cup heavy cream
- 2 tablespoons chopped fresh dill
- Kosher salt and freshly ground black pepper

---

1. Warm the butter or olive oil in a soup pot set over medium heat and sauté the onion and celery until translucent, about 5 minutes. Stir in the thyme and flour. Add the stock and saffron to the pot, bring the broth to a boil, then reduce the heat to medium low and simmer for 10 minutes, until slightly thickened. Carefully transfer the broth to a blender, puree until smooth, and pour it back into the pot, or use an immersion blender to puree it right in the pot.
2. Add the fish and corn kernels to the pureed broth and place the pot over medium-low heat. Simmer the soup for 5 minutes, until the fish is opaque and is easily flaked with a fork.
3. Finally, stir in the cream and dill, then season with salt and pepper and serve immediately.

APPLE LOAF CAKE

makes 1 loaf

This apple cake is an adaptation of my mom's pear bread recipe. A version of this sweet bread was originally published in my elementary school's PTA cookbook, which is a real treasure. Of course it's more of a cake than a bread, but the loaf is quick to put together and delicious no matter what you call it. My five-year-old daughter, Clara, loves to bake. She helps measure, mix, and chop and considers herself the "best egg cracker in the family." She's not wrong! I am happy to have her company in the kitchen, and even happier to see her excited about cooking and creating.

---

2 apples, pears, or a mixture of both, peeled, cored, and diced

2 teaspoons ground cinnamon

2 teaspoons plus ¾ cup pure cane sugar, divided

1 cup unbleached all-purpose flour

1½ teaspoons baking powder

½ teaspoon kosher salt

2 large eggs

¼ cup canola oil

¼ cup freshly squeezed orange juice

1½ teaspoon pure vanilla extract

---

1. Preheat the oven to 350°F. Grease a standard loaf pan.
2. In a small bowl, combine the diced fruit, cinnamon, and 2 teaspoons of the sugar. Toss to mix evenly and set aside.
3. Mix the flour, remaining ¾ cup of sugar, baking powder, and salt in a mixing bowl. In a separate bowl, whisk together the eggs, canola oil, orange juice, and vanilla. Gently stir the dry ingredients into the wet ingredients until everything is incorporated.
4. Pour two-thirds of the batter into the prepared pan. Top with the fruit mixture and then pour in the remaining batter. Bake the loaf for 45 to 60 minutes or until a testing stick comes out clean and the top and edges are golden brown. Remove the loaf from the oven, let it cool slightly, then slice and serve.

Roll 'Em Yourself

BUCKWHEAT CREPES WITH DELICATA SQUASH, BLACK BEANS, AND AVOCADO

When I was pregnant with Dylan, we lived within walking distance of a little café in Providence that is famous for their Roasted Butternut Squash Quesadillas. Needless to say, I frequented the place—waddling up the city sidewalk for yet another order of the satisfying meal. Ever since (and especially after we moved away), I find myself pulling the pieces of that beloved dish into our dinners. This meal allows everyone to build a crepe of their own—maybe someone chooses a simple avocado and cheese topping, while someone else only wants black beans. As far as I'm concerned, there is no wrong way to eat a hot, homemade buckwheat crepe.

BUCKWHEAT CREPES WITH DELICATA SQUASH, BLACK BEANS, AND AVOCADO

makes about 20 crepes (enough for tomorrow night, too) and enough filling for 8 crepes, serves 4

Here, delicata squash is rubbed with cumin and chili powder, roasted, and folded into a hot buckwheat crepe along with black beans, avocado, and cheese. The flavors are some of my favorites. Many pieces of this meal can be done ahead of time—roast the squash whenever you have a free thirty minutes. The blended crepe batter can wait for you in the fridge for up to twenty-four hours (just let it come to room temperature and give it a good stir before using).

KIDS CAN: Everyone can fill and fold their own crepes.

SQUASH

1 delicata squash

1 tablespoon olive oil

1 teaspoon ground cumin

½ teaspoon chili powder

Big pinch of kosher salt

CREPES

2 cups whole milk

1 tablespoon pure cane sugar

¼ teaspoon kosher salt

3 tablespoons unsalted butter, melted, plus more for cooking the crepes

½ cup buckwheat flour

¾ cup unbleached all-purpose flour

3 large eggs

FILLINGS

One 15-ounce can black beans, drained and rinsed

2 avocados, pitted and sliced

Shredded Monterey Jack or cheddar cheese

Hot sauce (optional)

---

1. Preheat the oven to 425°F.

2. Cut the squash in half lengthwise and scoop out the seeds, then cut it lengthwise again into 8 wedges. In a large bowl, toss the squash with the olive oil, cumin, chili powder, and salt. Arrange the spiced squash on a baking sheet, skin-side down, and roast for 30 minutes or until tender. Before you fill the crepes, peel the skin away from each piece of squash.

3. To make the crepe batter, combine all the ingredients in a blender and process until smooth.

4. When you're ready to cook, heat a 10-inch nonstick skillet over medium heat (you can use an official crepe pan, but you don't need to). Drop ½ teaspoon of unsalted butter in the hot pan and wipe it around with a spatula. Ladle ¼ cup of the batter into the middle of the hot skillet, swirling the pan to distribute the batter quickly

and evenly. After about 1 minute, run a spatula around the edge and bottom of the crepe, then flip it over. If you're topping the crepe with cheese, sprinkle the cheese on top at this point and cook for another 30 seconds, then slide it out onto a plate. Repeat, cooking the crepes with the remaining batter or until you have as many crepes as you like, stirring the batter every so often as you go.

5. I recommend eating the crepes as you go, since they are best right from the pan and take only take a minute to cook. As one family member fills their hot crepe, another one is done cooking. Fill the warm crepes with the roasted squash, black beans, avocado slices, and a dash of hot sauce (if you like). Crepes should be served warm. To reheat the crepes, fold them and put them in a covered baking dish in a warm oven.

FOR BABY: Smash a bowl of avocado, beans, and roasted squash for baby to enjoy. Older infants may like to hold a crepe and feed themselves, while younger eaters can try tiny torn bits.

TOMORROW'S DINNER: SWEET CREPES

The next evening, serve crepes with fresh fruit and yogurt.

Just 4 Ingredients

BEET AND POTATO HASH WITH EGGS

4-INGREDIENT PEANUT BUTTER BLOSSOM COOKIES

In my deep subconscious I must believe that eggs, root vegetables, and greens are meant to be together, because nine times out of ten my frazzled *we have nothing to eat for dinner* internal dialogue ends with eggs, potatoes, beets, and greens (of some sort) on our plates. This fearsome foursome of ingredients just happens to always be around when I need a quick meal and leaves my belly happy and satisfied time after time. For dessert, another simple list of ingredients (from the pantry this time) comes to the rescue—peanut butter, coconut sugar, eggs, and dark chocolate. I don't want to ruin the surprise, but together these make a quick cookie that is our best discovery to date.

BEET AND POTATO HASH WITH EGGS

serves 4

This one-pot hash is an ode to my fall root vegetable love. Add a runny egg yolk to the mix and forget about it. If you can, peel and dice the potatoes and beets the night before or the morning of the meal so that everything is waiting for you (diced root vegetables are best stored in a bowl of water in the fridge). If you love the earthy bite of meat in your hash, just sauté up some ground sausage, bacon, or pancetta to sprinkle over the finished skillet dinner. To make this a complete meal, I like to serve it with a simple green salad.

KIDS CAN: Helpers can peel the beets and potatoes.

---

1 pound beets (any color), peeled and cut into ½-inch dice

1½ pounds Yukon gold or Red Bliss potatoes, peeled (if they have thick skin), scrubbed, and cut into ½-inch dice

3 tablespoons extra virgin olive oil

1 small onion, finely chopped

1 teaspoon kosher salt, plus more as needed

2 tablespoons chopped fresh parsley

Freshly ground black pepper

4 large eggs

---

1. In a 12-inch cast iron skillet, cover the diced beets and potatoes with water and bring to a strong simmer over medium heat. Cook until the vegetables are tender, about 7 minutes, then drain them and wipe out the skillet.

2. Heat the oil in the same skillet over medium-high heat. Add the boiled beets and potatoes, the chopped onion, and 1 teaspoon of the salt. Cook until the potatoes begin to turn golden, about 8 minutes, tossing frequently. Stir in the parsley. Reduce the heat to medium. Make 4 wide wells in the hash. Crack 1 egg into each well and season the eggs with pinches of salt and grinds of pepper. Loosely cover the skillet with a sheet of aluminum foil. Continue to cook until the egg whites are set but the yolks are still runny, about 6 minutes. If the bottom of the hash appears to be cooking too quickly, turn the heat to medium low. Serve with a big bottle of hot sauce and a green salad.

FOR BABY: With the back of a fork, smash a few potatoes and beets for baby, then stir in soft bits of egg.

4-INGREDIENT PEANUT BUTTER BLOSSOM COOKIES

makes 24 small cookies

These cookies have only four ingredients and can be ready in ten minutes (enough said).

KIDS CAN: The simple ingredient list, dough rolling, and chocolate topping are perfect matches for small, eager hands.

---

1 cup creamy, honey-roasted (or regular) peanut butter or any seed butter

1 cup cocunut sugar

1 large egg

24 dark charcolate baking disks (large flat chocolate chips)

---

1. Preheat the oven to 350°F. Line a rimmed baking sheet with parchment paper.
2. In a medium bowl, whisk together the peanut butter, coconut sugar, and egg. Using a tablespoon measure, scoop up some of the batter and roll it between your palms until it is the size of a golf ball. Place the ball of dough on the prepared baking sheet and repeat with the remaining dough. You should have 24 balls. Top each dough ball with a disk of dark chocolate, place the baking sheet in the oven, and bake for 8 minutes, until the edges just start to darken. Remove the cookies from the oven and let them cool for 5 minutes on the baking sheet, then transfer them to a wire rack to cool completely.

FOR BABY: For babies comfortable with peanuts, leave a few balls plain (without the chocolate toppers) for a simple cookie.

GRAY

(Almost) Breakfast for Dinner

GERMAN APPLE PANCAKE WITH SHARP CHEDDAR

SHAVED BRUSSELS SPROUTS WITH BACON

When I was a kid, my mom would bake up a special breakfast she called German Apple Pancake on celebratory fall mornings (like my October birthday or vacation days around Thanksgiving). As an adult, I found myself making this hefty pancake for dinner—served with bacon, cheddar cheese, or greens. Here, I am pairing it with a quick side of shaved Brussels sprouts and bacon. Often I'll set the boys up with a few extra sprouts and encourage them to peel away the layers to investigate the insides of the vegetable. Sometime they sit, quiet and focused, for a good twenty minutes, taking care to look closely at their work. Other days, of course, they find that job totally unappealing, so I stick to the tried and true apple peeling and slicing task (with child-safe knives). Handheld metal tools for the win.

GERMAN APPLE PANCAKE WITH SHARP CHEDDAR

serves 4

This large, puffy pancake is made from a thin batter that is packed with eggs and butter surrounding thinly sliced apple. It is an easy one-skillet meal and comes out of the oven looking impressive and smelling even better.

KIDS CAN: Chefs of all ages can prepare the apples, then sit at the oven door and watch the pancake puff.

---

3 large eggs

¾ cup unbleached all-purpose flour

¾ cup whole milk

Pinch of kosher salt

3 tablespoons unsalted butter

1 apple, peeled and sliced into ¼-inch-thick slivers

½ cup shredded sharp cheddar cheese

---

1. Preheat the oven to 425°F.
2. In a large bowl, whisk together the eggs, flour, milk, and salt until everything is incorporated but the batter is still a little lumpy.
3. Melt the butter in a 10-inch ovenproof skillet over medium-high heat. Add the apple slices and cook until warmed, about 2 minutes. Pour in the batter and immediately transfer the skillet to the hot oven. Bake for 20 minutes, until the pancake is golden brown and rumpled looking. Remove the skillet from the oven and serve the pancake in wedges, piping hot, sprinkled with the cheddar cheese.

FOR BABY: Finely chop a serving of the apple pancake for baby to enjoy.

SHAVED BRUSSELS SPROUTS WITH BACON

serves 4

If you haven't tried shredding Brussels sprouts through your food processor, you should. The result is a pile of thin ribbons that cook quickly and don't take on any of that infamous mushy-Brussels sprout texture.

---

2 cups whole Brussels sprouts

3 strips of bacon

Pinch of kosher salt

---

1. Trim the Brussels sprouts (remove the bottom of the stems) and put them through a food processor fitted with the grater attachment. Set aside.
2. Chop the bacon and place it in a cast iron skillet set over medium heat. Cook the bacon until crisp, about 7 minutes. Remove the bacon bits from the pan and add in the shredded Brussels sprouts and a pinch of salt. Cook, tossing often, until the sprouts are soft and slightly browned, about 10 minutes. Stir in the crisp bacon and serve warm.

FOR BABY: If the Brussels sprout shavings are long and stringy, they may need to be minced or snipped with a pair of kitchen shears before serving to an infant.

Match Made in Heaven

CREAMY TOMATO AND SPINACH SOUP WITH GRILLED CHEESE CROUTONS

PEAR PIE IN CORNMEAL CRUST

Calling small bits of toasty grilled cheese "croutons" is really a tricky excuse to make a simple soup and sandwich dinner feel fun and different. Also, I find that the boys have a better soup-to-grilled cheese ratio when the grilled cheese is floating on top of the soup rather than sitting next to it.

CREAMY TOMATO AND SPINACH SOUP WITH GRILLED CHEESE CROUTONS

serves 6

I realize that there is a big world of creamy tomato soups out there, but I am head over heels for this one. It is extremely simple (essentially onions, tomatoes, and olive oil), is ready in about fifteen minutes, and has a deep, rich flavor. I often stir in a pile of baby spinach at the end (as I call for here), but you can add in almost anything, including small cooked pasta, precooked rice, white beans, or chickpeas.

KIDS CAN: Kids of every age can tear up the bread slices and spinach leaves for the soup.

SOUP

¼ cup olive oil, divided

2 garlic cloves, sliced

1 medium onion, sliced

1 teaspoon dried thyme

2 slices sandwich bread (whole wheat or white), crusts removed and roughly torn into ½-inch pieces

Two 28-ounce cans whole peeled tomatoes

1 teaspoon kosher salt, plus more as needed

2 cups baby spinach, roughly chopped or torn

Freshly ground black pepper

CROUTONS

4 slices whole wheat sandwich bread

2 tablespoons unsalted butter, at room temperature

4 to 6 slices sharp cheddar cheese

1. Heat 2 tablespoons of the olive oil in a large soup pot over medium heat. Add the garlic, onion, and thyme to the pot and cook, stirring frequently, until the onions are softened but not browned, about 4 minutes. Add in the torn bread and tomatoes. Roughly mash the tomatoes with a potato masher.
2. Pour in 2 cups of water and add the salt. Bring the soup to a boil over high heat, reduce the heat to medium, and simmer for 5 minutes, then reduce the heat to low.
3. Using an immersion blender (or stand blender), blend the soup until the large bits of tomato and bread are pureed. If you used a stand blender, return the soup to the pot. Stir in the remaining 2 tablespoons of olive oil and the spinach leaves. Cook for 5 more minutes over low heat or until the spinach leaves are just wilted.
4. To make the croutons, butter one side of each slice of bread. Layer cheese slices across two slices, then top with the remaining bread. Toast in a pan over medium heat until golden on both sides (flipping when appropriate). Roughly chop the warm sandwiches to make "croutons." Ladle the soup into individual serving bowls and top with grilled cheese croutons.

FOR BABY: A hefty serving of tomatoes can be too acidic for little bellies. Instead of offering baby a bowl of soup, spoon a few tablespoons of the creamy tomato soup over a bowl of rice.

PEAR PIE IN CORNMEAL CRUST

serves 8

Years ago I made a version of this pie to celebrate my dad's November birthday, as he is not a fluffy cake type of guy. This hearty and subtly sweet dessert was perfect and has appeared in our kitchen every fall since then. The dough can be made a few days ahead of time and stored in the refrigerator until you are ready to assemble and bake the pie. If you are short on pears but heavy on apples, feel free to bake this pie with half pears and half apples.

KIDS CAN: Little helpers can peel and slice the pears, help roll out the dough, and crimp the pie edges.

CRUST

2 cups unbleached all-purpose flour

½ cup yellow cornmeal

1 teaspoon kosher salt

1 cup (2 sticks) cold unsalted butter, cut into small pieces

¼ cup ice water

FILLING

5 pears (I use Bartlett), cored, peeled (optional), and cut into ½-inch-thick slices

1 teaspoon ground cinnamon

1 tablespoon arrowroot powder

3 tablespoons packed brown sugar (light or dark)

Pinch of kosher salt

Juice of ½ lemon

1 large egg, beaten, for brushing

1 tablespoon coarse sugar, for topping

Vanilla ice cream or whipped cream, for serving (optional)

---

1. To make the crust, combine the flour, cornmeal, and salt in the bowl of a food processor and pulse a few times to mix. Add the cubed butter and pulse 10 times to form large crumbs. Next, with the motor running, slowly stream in the cold water through the feed tube until the dough comes away from the sides of the bowl and begins to form a ball. Turn the dough onto a floured counter and divide it in half. Shape the two mounds into 1-inch-thick disks. Wrap the disks tightly in plastic and refrigerate for at least 1 hour and up to 48 hours.
2. When you're ready to assemble the pie, preheat the oven to 400°F. Flour a work surface and roll out each disk of dough into a 12-inch circle.
3. To make the filling, in a large bowl, toss the pear slices with the cinnamon, arrowroot powder, brown sugar, salt, and lemon juice.
4. Lay one rolled piece of dough in the bottom of an 8-inch pie dish, pressing to fit the dough into the edges and up the sides of the dish. Spoon the filling into the dough-lined pie dish and top with the second piece of rolled dough. Trim any excess crust hanging over the pan and

crimp the edges with your fingers or fork tines. Cut a few slits in the top of the pie so steam can escape.

5. Brush the top of the pie with the beaten egg and sprinkle with the coarse sugar. Bake for 20 minutes, reduce the oven temperature to 350°F, and bake for another 30 to 40 minutes, until the crust is lightly golden and the juices are bubbling. Remove the pie from the oven and let it cool on a wire rack for 30 minutes, then serve with vanilla ice cream or whipped cream, if desired.

FOR BABY: Younger infants may enjoy a few slices of soft pear from the pie, while older babies can try bits of the crust as well.

For the First Frost

CHEESY BUTTERNUT SQUASH CASSEROLE

MAPLE-TAPIOCA PUDDING

This casserole is something I put together when I have a free chunk of time, either over the weekend or in the evening, and then I stick the whole thing in the refrigerator. On a night when there is just no time to cook, we pull it out of the fridge and toss it in a hot oven for a hands-off dinner. If the kids are around when I am prepping the squash, I put them in charge of scooping out and cleaning the seeds. Butternut squash seeds are delicious tossed in oil and salt and toasted in the oven, just like their old cousin the pumpkin. Before bed, cups of make-ahead Maple Tapioca Pudding soften the mental blow that winter is, inevitably, just around the corner.

CHEESY BUTTERNUT SQUASH CASSEROLE

serves 6

You can serve this dish with a big skillet of garlicky greens, grilled chicken sausages, chicken thighs, or really whatever you like. Depending on the hectic-ness of your week, you can either prepare the recipe ahead of time through step one or step two (just short of baking), or complete it entirely so all you have to do is reheat the meal for dinner. If your family is sweet on sweet potatoes, you can easily substitute in the (vitamin C–packed) orange potatoes for the (vitamin A–packed) orange squash.

KIDS CAN: Ask your helpers to scoop squash seeds, chop herbs, and help layer the casserole.

¼ cup (½ stick) unsalted butter, plus more for greasing the casserole dish

3 medium yellow onions, peeled and quartered

One 2½-pound butternut squash, peeled, seeded, and cut into ½-inch cubes

1 teaspoon kosher salt

¾ cup low-sodium chicken broth (or vegetable broth)

2 cups panko bread crumbs

2 cups (6 ounces) shredded Gruyère cheese

2½ teaspoons chopped fresh rosemary

½ teaspoon chopped fresh thyme

7 grinds of black pepper

---

1. Preheat the oven to 350°F. Butter a casserole dish.

2. Thinly slice the onions using the food processor's slicing blade. Melt the butter in a large skillet over medium-high heat, add the sliced onions, and sauté until the onions are soft and golden, about 8 minutes. Add the cubed squash and salt and cook for 5 minutes more, until the squash begins to soften.

3. Transfer the vegetable mixture to the prepared casserole pan. Pour the broth over the squash and onions. Cover the dish tightly with aluminum foil and bake for 45 minutes. Remove the casserole from the oven and increase the oven temperature to 400°F.

4. In a small bowl, mix together the bread crumbs, cheese, rosemary, thyme, and pepper. Carefully remove the foil from the casserole and sprinkle on the topping. Return the casserole to the oven and bake, uncovered, for 30 minutes, until the top is golden and crisp. Remove and let stand for 10 minutes before serving.

FOR BABY: Smash a small serving of cooled casserole with the back of a fork for easy eating.

MAPLE-TAPIOCA PUDDING

serves 6

This simple, make-ahead pudding is thickened with full-fat coconut milk and can be topped with anything from fresh mango chunks to dark chocolate shavings.

KIDS CAN: Everyone can add their favorite toppings to their cups of tapioca pudding.

---

3 cups full-fat coconut milk (from 2 cans)

¼ cup quick-cooking tapioca

Pinch of kosher salt

1 teaspoon pure vanilla extract

3 tablespoons pure maple syrup, plus more for serving

---

1. In a medium saucepan, whisk the coconut milk to break up any chunks of cream, then bring it to a boil over medium-high heat. Stir in the tapioca and salt and reduce the heat to medium low. Simmer for 15 minutes, stirring often and taking special care to make sure the tapioca pieces are not sticking to the bottom of the pan, until the pearls are plump and translucent.

2. Turn off the heat and stir in the vanilla and maple syrup. Transfer the pudding to a bowl, cover, and refrigerate for about 2 hours or until it comes to room temperature. Serve with extra maple syrup and other toppings of your choice, such as chopped fruit, toasted unsweetened coconut, dark chocolate chunks, or nuts.

FOR BABY: This naturally sweetened pudding is a special, creamy treat for baby.

Fall Sunday Supper (And a Donut Party Game)

AUTUMN MEATBALL SUBS

BROCCOLI SLAW

BAKED APPLE CIDER DONUTS

Everyone loves a hearty meatball sub, and having a skillet of meatballs on the stove at 4:30 P.M. on a fall Sunday feels just about perfect. Maybe you make these for the big game or to have something stowed away in the back of the fridge for the overwhelmingly hectic week ahead. In either case, you'll thank yourself. The meatballs are made from a mix of ground turkey and pork, and are speckled with shreds of apples and carrots. I like these sandwiches with a pile of Broccoli Slaw, a simple salad that can be made up to twenty-four hours ahead of time. For dessert I'm sharing our recipe for Baked Apple Cider Donuts. As I have an October birthday, the entertainment at my childhood parties was in the form of bobbing for apples, pumpkin carving, and trying to catch bites of spiced donuts hanging from strings (no hands!). If you happen to host a fall party or just want something special to do over the weekend, tie these little beauties to a low hanging branch and let the kids go at it. Perhaps while you sip a pumpkin ale nearby? Happy fall.

AUTUMN MEATBALL SUBS

serves 5; makes 15 medium-size meatballs

To freeze extra cooked meatballs (either leftovers or those made from a double batch), first arrange them in a single layer on a baking sheet. Place the baking sheet in the freezer, and when the meatballs are completely frozen, pile them into a big storage bag. This method insures that the meatballs don't stick together. To defrost, simply transfer the meatballs to the fridge in the morning. At dinnertime, warm the already browned meat in tomato sauce until heated through.

KIDS CAN: For a fun and messy project, invite the kids to roll out the meatballs with you.

- ¾ pound ground turkey
- ¾ pound ground pork
- 2 tablespoons plus 1 teaspoon olive oil, divided
- 1 small yellow onion, finely chopped
- 1 garlic clove, minced
- ½ medium apple, peeled and grated
- 1 medium carrot, peeled and grated
- ½ cup finely ground fresh bread crumbs
- ¼ cup whole milk
- ½ teaspoon ground cumin
- 1 teaspoon kosher salt
- 8 grinds of black pepper
- 2 tablespoons finely chopped parsley
- 2 cups favorite marinara sauce
- 4 long French rolls, split
- Parmesan cheese, for serving

---

1. Combine the turkey and pork in a mixing bowl.
2. Heat 1 teaspoon of the olive oil in a saucepan over medium-high heat. Add the onion, garlic, apple, and carrot; cook briefly until wilted, about 5 minutes. Remove the pan from the heat and set it aside.
3. Combine the bread crumbs and milk in a large bowl. Add the meat, onion and apple mixture, cumin, salt, pepper, and parsley. Mix well. Roll the mixture into golf ball–size rounds and set them aside. You should have 15 meatballs.
4. Heat the remaining 2 tablespoons of olive oil in a large skillet over medium-high heat. Add the meatballs, cook for 5 minutes, then flip them and cook for another 5 minutes or until browned. Add the marinara sauce to the skillet and bring it to a simmer, then cover and cook for about 10 minutes or until the sauce has thickened slightly.
5. To serve, toast the rolls and brush the insides with a little olive oil. Pile the meatballs and sauce into the toasted rolls, top with some Parmesan, and enjoy.

FOR BABY: Crumble a lightly sauced meatball for baby to enjoy. Serve with a few raisins and pine nuts from the slaw on the next page.

TOMORROW'S DINNER: SPAGHETTI AND MEATBALLS

Leftover meatballs can be served with spaghetti or roughly chopped and baked into a cheesy ziti casserole.

BROCCOLI SLAW

serves 4

This is a perfect make-ahead side, as the salad's sturdiness allows it to sit in the fridge for up to twenty-four hours without becoming soggy. I love using the food processor's slicing blade to prepare the broccoli and shallot—the result is thin wisps of vegetables (including those "I don't know what to do with" broccoli stems) without any time-consuming knife work.

SLAW

¼ cup pine nuts

1 large head of broccoli

1 small shallot (or ½ yellow onion), peeled

⅓ cup raisins

DRESSING

¼ cup plain full-fat Greek yogurt

¼ cup buttermilk

1½ teaspoons apple cider vinegar

½ teaspoon pure cane sugar

1 teaspoon Worcestershire sauce

½ teaspoon kosher salt

A few grinds of black pepper

---

1. To make the slaw, first toast the pine nuts in a dry skillet over medium heat.
2. Cut the broccoli florets off the stem and cut the stem into large chunks. Thinly slice the shallot using your food processor's slicing blade, then do the same with the broccoli florets and stem. Transfer the sliced shallot and broccoli to a large bowl and toss in the pine nuts and raisins.
3. To make the dressing, whisk together all the ingredients in a small bowl.
4. Pour the dressing over the broccoli slaw and toss well. Taste, add more salt or pepper as needed, then cover the bowl and refrigerate for at least 1 hour before serving. The slaw can be made up to 1 day ahead.

BAKED APPLE CIDER DONUTS

makes 12 donuts

As far as I'm concerned, a family living in the Northeast can't survive the fall without a steady stream of cider donuts. I think the spicy fall flavors and subtle sweetness of this classic donut is in my blood, as my parents spent many of their first dates in the 1970s eating cider donuts at a farm in western Massachusetts. I know donuts seem like unattainable desserts for home cooks, but with a modest donut pan investment you can bake up different flavor combinations all year long.

KIDS CAN: Who doesn't love to sprinkle donuts with cinnamon and sugar? Invite the kids to the party.

---

3 tablespoons canola oil, plus more for brushing the pan

2 cups unbleached all-purpose flour

1½ teaspoons baking powder

1½ teaspoons baking soda

½ teaspoon kosher salt

2 teaspoons ground cinnamon

1 large egg, beaten

⅔ cup coconut sugar

½ cup apple butter

⅓ cup pure maple syrup

⅓ cup spiced apple cider

⅓ cup plain full-fat yogurt

TOPPINGS (OPTIONAL)

2 tablespoons pure maple syrup

2 to 3 tablespoons ground cinnamon

¼ cup pure cane sugar

---

1. Preheat the oven to 400°F. Brush a donut pan with canola oil. (If you don't have a donut pan, these also make yummy mini muffins or small loaf cakes.)
2. In a mixing bowl, whisk together the flour, baking powder, baking soda, salt, and cinnamon. In a separate bowl, whisk together the egg, coconut sugar, apple butter, maple syrup, cider, yogurt, and 3 tablespoons of canola oil. Add the dry ingredients to the wet ingredients and stir until just moistened.
3. Spoon 2 tablespoons of batter into each donut round (don't fill to the top or it will overflow).
4. Bake the donuts for 10 minutes, until puffed and golden brown. Invert the donuts onto a wire rack to cool. Wipe out the pan and then re-coat it with canola oil. Repeat the process to make a total of 12 donuts.
5. For a special topping, brush the baked donuts with maple syrup and sprinkle them with a mixture of cinnamon and sugar.

FOR BABY: Reserve a plain donut (before dusting with cinnamon and sugar) for baby to hold or try crumbs from.

With Gratitude

Thank you to Dylan and Gray for being just exactly how you are.

Thank you to my husband, Nick, for always encouraging me to go big. I can't help but smile thinking of us flipping through this book years from now, reminiscing on what a crazy and wonderful time of life this was. I am so happy to be living it with you.

Thank you to my parents for your limitless commitment and generosity to my family and me. I am so very grateful for everything you do for us (including eating many of these meals). Thank you to my sister Anna for thirty-two years of companionship. I don't know what I'd do without you.

Thank you to my lifelong girlfriends, those whom I have grown up with. Your friendships mean the world to me. Thank you to my island friends for reminding me (even when I'm stuck in a little kitchen on a little island in the middle of February with two very eager helpers at my feet) that this is a very cool job—one I'm lucky to have. Thank you for taking leftovers again and again.

Thank you to Elizabeth Cecil for capturing the perfect images to match our story. Your eagle eye, class, and good humor made this project fun from start to finish.

Thank you to my editor, Jennifer Urban-Brown, for your graceful guidance in shaping this book. And to the whole Roost family, thank you for inviting me to be on your killer team.

Thank you to the Moriarty family, Solon family, Hay family, and Kenner family for sharing your food, family, and time with us. Thank you to the Thomson family for participating in a spontaneous donut party and to the Coutts family for roasting marshmallows out in the cold.

Thank you to the teachers at The Chilmark Preschool and The Chilmark School for loving and nurturing first Dylan and then Gray while I sat at the kitchen table (and stove) making this book.

And last, but most important, thank you to the people everywhere doing their best to feed those they love. This is a hard job and you are doing great, important work.

Index

C

ABOUT THE AUTHOR

SARAH WALDMAN fell in love with food while playing "cooking show" with her little sister in the 1980s. Decades later, she followed that passion to the Institute of Integrative Nutrition to study the connections between food and personal wellness. Now Sarah spends her time being a mother, food writer, and recipe developer. As a health-focused home cook, she develops and offers recipes for simple, whole-food meals appropriate for every member of the family. Her work has been featured in *Fine Cooking*, *Shape*, *Edible Vineyard*, *Food 52*, and the *Coastal Table*. Sarah lives on Martha's Vineyard with her husband and two boys. On her blog (Sarah Waldman.com) she shares healthy, seasonal recipes that celebrate a family-focused life.

ABOUT THE PHOTOGRAPHER

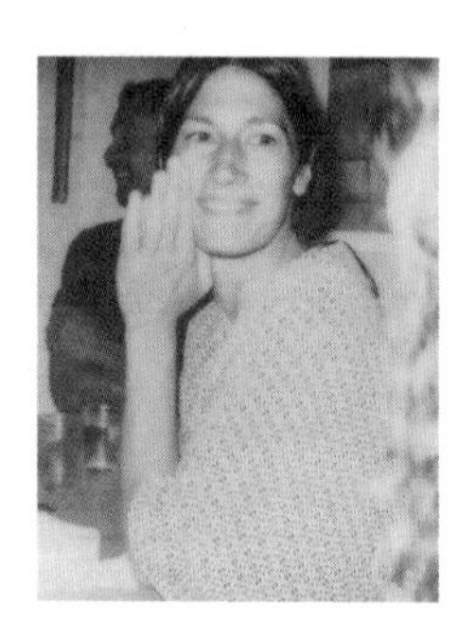

ELIZABETH CECIL is a professional photographer. Whether she is shooting food, lifestyle, or travel, her work is inspired by light, color, and her natural surroundings. Elizabeth aims to capture visual authenticity and poetry in everything she photographs. Her work has appeared in *Bon Appétit*, *Saveur*, *Coastal Living*, and the *Wall Street Journal*. She is a contributing photographer and the founding photo editor of *Edible Vineyard*. When she's not making pictures, you can find her out catching waves with her husband or in the kitchen baking a pie. Elizabeth lives on the island of Martha's Vineyard except when she boards the ferry or hops on a plane to travel for work.